# Attack
## of the
## 50 Foot
## Blockchain

HILLSBORO PUBLIC LIBRARIES
Hillsboro, OR
Member of Washington County
COOPERATIVE LIBRARY SERVICES

WITHDRAWN

WITHDRAWN

# Attack
## of the
## 50 Foot
## Blockchain

### Bitcoin, Blockchain,
### Ethereum and Smart Contracts

## David Gerard

2

Copyright © 2017 David Gerard. All rights reserved. No part of this book may be reproduced or transmitted in any form or by any means, electronic or mechanical, including photocopying, recording, or by any information storage and retrieval system without the written permission of the author, except where permitted by law.

A Bitcoin FAQ © 2013 Christian Wagner, used with permission. (This section is also available for reuse under Creative Commons Attribution-NonCommercial-ShareAlike 3.0 Unported [cc-by-nc-sa].)

"Stages in a Bubble" © 2008 Jean-Paul Rodrigue, released by the author for any reuse with attribution.

Skunk House photograph © 2016 Karen Boyd, used with permission.

Mr. Bitcoin photograph © 2014 Ben Gutzler, used with permission.

Mining rig photograph of unknown origin; if this is yours, please get in touch.

First edition, July 2017
ISBN-13 (print): 978-1974000067

Book site: www.davidgerard.co.uk/blockchain
Contact the author: dgerard@gmail.com

Cover art and design: Alli Kirkham www.punkpuns.com/author

# Contents

# A Bitcoin FAQ

© Christian Wagner

http://brokenlibrarian.org/bitcoin/

**Short Version**

1) *Should I buy Bitcoins?*

No.

2) *But I keep seeing all this stuff in the news about them and how*

No. Tech journalism is uniformly terrible, always remember this.

3) *How does this work? It doesn't make any sense!*

No, it really doesn't. It's impossible to accurately explain Bitcoin in anything less than mind-numbingly boring technical terms so you should probably just not worry about it. Go do something useful instead.

# Introduction

**Abstract:** A purely peer-to-peer version of electronic cash would allow online payments to be sent directly from one party to another without going through a financial institution.

– Satoshi Nakamoto, *Bitcoin: A Peer-to-Peer Electronic Cash System,* 2008[1]

An experimental new Internet-based form of money is created that anyone can generate at home. People build frightening firetrap computers full of video cards, putting out so much heat that one operator is hospitalised with heatstroke and brain damage.

Someone known only as "Pirateat40" starts a "high yield investment program." Just before its collapse as a Ponzi scheme, it holds 7% of all bitcoins at the time. Aggrieved investors eventually manage to convince the authorities not only that these Internet tokens are worth anything, but that they gave them to some guy on an Internet forum calling himself "Pirate" because he said he would double their money.

A young physics student starts a revolutionary new marketplace based on the nonaggression principle, immune to State coercion. He ends up ordering hits on people because they might threaten his great experiment, and is jailed for life without parole.

A legal cryptographer proposes fully automated contractual systems that run with minimal human interference, so that business and the law will work better and be more trusted. The contracts people actually write are automated Ponzi schemes, though they later progress to unregulated penny stock offerings whose fine print literally states that you are buying nothing of any value.

The biggest crowdfunding in history attracts $150 million on the promise that it will embody "the steadfast iron will of *unstoppable code.*" Upon release it is immediately hacked, and $50 million is stolen.

Bitcoin's good name having been somewhat stained by drugs and criminals, its advocates try to sell the technology to business as "Blockchain." $1.5 billion of venture capital gets back, so far, zero. The main visible product is consultant hours and press releases.

How did we get here?

Digital cash, without having to check in with a central authority, is obviously a useful idea. It turned out in practice to be a magnet for enthusiastic amateurs with stars in their eyes and con artists to prey upon them, with outcomes both hilarious and horrifying.

Bitcoin and blockchains are not a technology story, but a psychology story: bubble economy thinking and the art of the steal.

Despite the creators' good intentions, the cryptocurrency field is replete with scams and scammers. The technology is used as an excuse to make outlandish near-magical claims. When phrases like "a whole new form of money" or "the old rules don't apply any more" start going around, people get gullible and the ethically-challenged get creative.

You can make money from Bitcoin! But it is *vastly more likely* that you will be the one that others make *their* money from.

Remember: if it sounds too good to be true, it almost certainly is.


In this book, I cover the origins and history of Bitcoin to the present day, with some of the important stories, the other cryptocurrencies it spawned – particularly Ethereum – and smart contracts and the attempts to apply blockchains to business. There's also a case study on blockchains in the music industry.

I go into technical detail where it's relevant, though what's more important are the implications. There are also extensive footnotes, with links in the digital edition to the sources for further reading, and a glossary.

# Chapter 1: What is a bitcoin?

## Why Bitcoin?

Paper notes and metal coins are annoying and inconvenient, and we have the Internet now. So digital money sounds like a useful idea.

The solution the developed world has mostly come to is just using our banks – you have an account, and you can move money to other people's accounts, via debit card, credit card, PayPal or whatever. The central authority means it's sensibly regulated, errors and thefts can be reversed and so on. It's also a smooth transition from paper money – the same thing, but you can do new things with it.

But this isn't a complete solution; a shop's card reader could be down, your payment gateway might charge fees, you may want to send money to someone not on the same banking network, you value your privacy, checking in with your bank every time gets annoying. So a form of digital cash would be nice too.

Bitcoin is a *cryptocurrency:* a thing on the Internet which lets you exchange unique digital objects. The objects would take approximately forever to fake; so if we assign the objects a value, we can exchange them in a manner something like we do money. It's decentralised, so you can send money without having to go through a central clearing house.

Bitcoin's transaction ledger, the *blockchain,* is touted as *immutable:* nobody can alter it without it being obvious that it was tampered with. The idea is that there's no central control, anyone can run a Bitcoin node and be part of the network, nobody can block or reverse your transactions and you don't have to take *anyone's* word for the state of the system.

## What you have when you have "a bitcoin"

You know what feels like "money" to you. You can earn it, you can spend it on all manner of things, you can save it for the future, you can invest it. It might be in a bank account with a card, or notes and coins in your pocket – it still feels like a pound or a dollar to you.

In practice, bitcoins are a bit like money in a bank account with a debit card, except without any sort of safety net – it's all unregulated and uninsured, there's no way to reverse a transaction, and there's no customer service.

If you "have" bitcoins, you don't actually have them as things on your computer. What you've got is a Bitcoin *address* (like a bank account number) and the *key* to that address (another number, which works like the PIN to the first number).* The Bitcoin address is mentioned in transactions on the blockchain; the key is the unique thing you have that makes your bitcoins yours.

To send bitcoins from your address to another address (a bit like sending money over PayPal), you generate a transaction that is sent out into the network and added to the next block of transactions. Once it's in a block, that transaction is publicly visible on the blockchain forever.

A *wallet* is where you keep your keys. Usually it's a program which generates and manages addresses, and presents you with the balances. You can generate a new address, and its matching key, any time you like.

You can keep your bitcoins' keys in a *hot wallet* (like a current account), running on a computer attached to the Internet, or in a *cold wallet* (like keeping money in a sock under your bed), which might be on a computer not attached to the Internet, or could just be the keys themselves stored on a USB stick or even printed out on paper.

If you lose the key, your bitcoins are lost forever. If someone else gets the key, they can take your bitcoins. If you send bitcoins to a nonexistent address, they're lost forever. If you send bitcoins to the wrong address, you can't reverse it. Bitcoin security can be very technical, difficult and unforgiving; most people just keep their bitcoins on an exchange. These have their own problems, as we'll see later.

---

* This is *public key cryptography*, where the address is the "public key" (that everyone knows) and the key is the "private key" (that only you know), which are a matched pair: a message encrypted with one key can be decrypted with the other.

# The blockchain

Bitcoin transactions are grouped into blocks. Each block has a cryptographic *hash*, a number which is quickly calculated and serves as a check value – like the last digit of a book's ISBN, or the last digit of your credit card, but longer – to verify that a chunk of data is the chunk you think it is.

The hash will be completely different if there's even the slightest change in the data; as such, two things with the same hash are routinely assumed to be identical.

Advocates describe Bitcoin as "secured by math." This is because cryptography works on arithmetic that is fast going forward and impossibly slow to reverse – to make another data chunk with the same hash, you would have to go through a stupendous number of possible values. (Bitcoin mining relies on this – see below.)

Each block is also hashed with the chain of previous blocks, so the entire chain of blocks is tamper-evident. This is called a *Merkle tree*, invented in 1979 and widely used since.[*] What Bitcoin does is make possible a tamper-evident public ledger of transactions, without any central authority declaring whose ledger is the official one.

The Bitcoin blockchain contains every confirmed transaction back to January 2009. In June 2017 it passed 120 gigabytes and is growing at 4GB a month.

# Secured by waste: Proof of Work

So how do you decide who gets to write to the ledger? The answer is: competitive Proof of Work, where you waste computing power to demonstrate your commitment.[†]

A new block of transactions is created every ten minutes or so, with 12.5 bitcoins (BTC[‡]) reward attached as incentive, plus any fees on the transactions. Bitcoin *miners* (analogous to gold miners) apply as

---

[*]  Technically a Merkle tree is only the tree of hashes within a block, but cryptocurrency routinely uses the term to describe a chain of hashes as well.

[†]  Though you only hear about it these days in regard to cryptocurrency, Proof of Work was first mooted in 1992 to deal with email spam: Cynthia Dwork, Moni Daor. "Pricing via Processing or Combatting Junk Mail". In *Proceedings of the 12th Annual International Cryptology Conference on Advances in Cryptology* (CRYPTO '92), Ernest F. Brickell (Ed.). Springer-Verlag, London, UK, 139-147.

much brute-force computing power as they can to take the prize in this block's cryptographic lottery.

(The mining reward halves every four years – it started at 50 BTC, went to 25 BTC in 2012 and 12.5 BTC in 2016 – and will stop entirely in 2140. There will only ever be 21 million bitcoins.)

Satoshi Nakamoto, Bitcoin's creator, needed a task that people could compete to waste computing power on, that would give one winner every ten minutes. The difficulty would need to automatically adjust, as computing power joined and left, to keep block creation steady at about one every ten minutes.

What he came up with was: Unprocessed transactions are broadcast across the Bitcoin network. A miner collects together a block of transactions and the hash of the last known block. They add an arbitrary "nonce" value, then calculate the hash of the resulting block. If that hash satisfies the current difficulty criterion, they have mined a block! This successful block is then broadcast to the network, who can quickly verify the block is valid. The miner gets 12.5 BTC plus the transaction fees. If they failed, they pick another nonce value and try again.[2]

Since it's all but impossible to pick what data will have a particular hash, guessing what value will give a valid block takes many calculations – as of June 2017 the Bitcoin network was running 5,500,000,000,000,000,000 ($5.5 \times 10^{18}$, or 5.5 quintillion) hashes per second, or $3.3 \times 10^{21}$ (3.3 sextillion) per ten minutes.

The 3.3 sextillion calculations are thrown away, because the only point of all this technical rigmarole is to show that you can waste electricity faster than everyone else.

Obviously, the competition gets viciously Darwinian very quickly. Mining rapidly converges on 1 BTC costing 1 BTC to generate. The ensuing evolutionary arms race, as miners desperately try for enough of an edge to turn a profit, is such that Bitcoin's power usage is on the order of the entire power consumption of Ireland.[3]

This electricity is literally wasted for the sake of decentralisation; the power cost to confirm the transactions and add them to the blockchain is around $10-20 per transaction. That's not imaginary money – those are actual dollars, or these days mostly Chinese yuan, coming from people buying the new coins and going to pay for the electricity. An ordinary centralised database could calculate an equally

---

‡    More properly, "XBT" (a currency without an official symbol should be named starting with an X), though most people use "BTC" anyway.

tamper-evident block of transactions on a 2007 smartphone running off USB power. Even if Bitcoin could replace conventional currencies, it would be an ecological disaster.

So why bother with all of this? Ideology. From day one, Bitcoin was about pushing politics.

# Chapter 2: The Bitcoin ideology

> At first, almost everyone who got involved did so for philosophical reasons. We saw bitcoin as a great idea, as a way to separate money from the state.
>
> – Roger Ver[4]

The Bitcoin ideology propagated through two propositions:
- if you want to get rich for free, take on this weird ideology;
- don't worry if you don't understand the ideology yet, just keep *doing the things* and you'll get rich for free!

The promise of getting rich for free is enough to get people to take on the ideas that they're told makes it all work. Bitcoin went heavily political very fast, and Bitcoin partisans promoted anarcho-capitalism (yes, those two words can in fact go together), with odd notions of how economics works or humans behave, from the start.

The roots of the Bitcoin ideology go back through libertarianism, anarcho-capitalism and Austrian economics to the "end the Fed" and "establishment elites" conspiracy theories of the John Birch Society and Eustace Mullins. The design of Bitcoin and the political tone of its early community make sense only in the context of the extremist ideas ancestral to the cyberlibertarian subculture it arose from.[*] Most of Bitcoin's problems as money are because it's built on crank assumptions.

## Libertarianism and cyberlibertarianism

Libertarianism is a simple idea: freedom is good and government is bad. The word "libertarian" originally meant communist and anarchist activists in 19th-century France. The American right-wing variant starts at fairly normal people who want less bureaucracy and regulation and consider lower taxes more important than social spending. The seriously ideological ones go rather further – *e.g.*,

---

[*] This section draws from *The Politics of Bitcoin: Software as Right-Wing Extremism* by David Golumbia (University of Minnesota Press, 2016).

anarcho-capitalism, the belief in the supremacy of property rights and the complete elimination of the state.

American-style libertarians abound on the Internet. Computer programmers are highly susceptible to the just world fallacy (that their economic good fortune is the product of virtue rather than circumstance) and the fallacy of transferable expertise (that being competent in one field means they're competent in others). Silicon Valley has always been a cross of the hippie counterculture and Ayn Rand-based libertarianism (this cross being termed the "Californian ideology").

"Cyberlibertarianism" is the academic term for the early Internet strain of this ideology. Technological expertise is presumed to trump all other forms of expertise, *e.g.*, economics or finance, let alone softer sciences. "I don't understand it, but it must be simple" is the order of the day.

The implicit promise of cyberlibertarianism was the dot-com era promise that you could make it big from a startup company's Initial Public Offering: build something new and useful, suddenly get rich from it. The explicit promise of Bitcoin is that you can get in early and get rich – without even building an enterprise that's useful to someone.

## Pre-Bitcoin anonymous payment channels

Peer-to-peer electronic payment services existed before Bitcoin. PayPal was explicitly intended to be an anonymous regulation-dodging money transmission channel, with an anti-state ideology; in a 1999 motivational speech to employees, Peter Thiel rants how "it will be nearly impossible for corrupt governments to steal wealth from their people through their old means"[5] – though they quickly realised that being part of the system made for a much more viable business.

e-Gold was a digital currency backed by gold, founded in 1996. It was perceived as anonymous but was actually pseudonymous, and the company made their records available to law enforcement. It was quite popular before being shut down in 2009 for not having obtained a money transmitter's license in the previous several years.

Liberty Reserve in Costa Rica operated from 2006 to 2013. It was all about the anonymous money transmission, and founder Arthur Budovsky (who had previously been convicted for running a similar operation in the US) ended up jailed for 20 years for money laundering. Some Bitcoiners regarded Liberty Reserve as a predecessor to Bitcoin and worried at the possible precedent this might set.[6]

# The prehistory of cryptocurrencies

Cryptographic money was first mooted by David Chaum in his 1982 paper "Blind Signatures for Untraceable Payments"[7] and his 1985 paper "Security without Identification: Transaction Systems to Make Big Brother Obsolete."[8] Chaum founded DigiCash in 1990 to put his ideas into practice. It failed in the market, however, and closed in 1998.

Most concepts later used in Bitcoin originated on the Cypherpunks mailing list in the early 1990s. The ideology was libertarian right-wing anarchism, often explicitly labeled anarcho-capitalism; they considered government interference the gravest possible threat, and hoped to fight it off using the new cryptographic techniques invented in the 1970s and 1980s. They also tied into the Silicon Valley and Bay Area Extropian/transhumanist subculture. Tim May's "Crypto Anarchist Manifesto," a popular document on the list, is all about the promise of money and commerce with no government oversight, and anticipates many of the future promises and aspirations of cryptocurrency.[9]

Chaum's DigiCash was not acceptable to the Cypherpunks, as a single company confirmed every participant's signature. They wanted something that didn't rely on a central authority in any way.

Adam Back proposed Hashcash to the list in 1997, money created by guessing the reversal of a cryptographic hash; Nick Szabo put forward Bitgold and Wei Dai b-money in 1998. These were all bare proposals, without working implementations.

"Cypherpunk" was a pun on "cyberpunk." Cyberpunk science fiction of the 1980s never got much into pure bank-free cryptographic currencies; it mostly treated the idea of transmitting money digitally at all as being interesting enough for story purposes. (If William Gibson had thought of Bitcoin for his cyber-heist short "Burning Chrome," it could have been set in the present day.) The Cypherpunks got very excited about Neal Stephenson's 1999 novel *Cryptonomicon*, one plot thread of which involves a fictional sultanate promoting a cryptographic digital currency, even though the book example is issued by a government and backed by gold.

An anonymous person calling himself "Satoshi Nakamoto" started working on Bitcoin in 2007,[10] as a completely trustless implementation of the b-money and Bitgold proposals[11] (though Nakamoto wasn't aware of Szabo's work until quite late in the process).[12] In 2008, he emailed Adam Back with some of his ideas, and six weeks later announced the Bitcoin white paper on the Cryptography and Cryptography Policy mailing list, a successor to the Cypherpunks list. It was, at last, a proposal with a plausible decentralisation mechanism, soon followed by actual working code that people could try. Nakamoto and list contributor Hal Finney tested the software in November and December 2008, and Bitcoin 0.1 was released in January 2009.

## The conspiracy theory economics of Bitcoin

The *gold standard* – an economy with a finite money supply – was accepted mainstream monetary policy up to the early 20th century, when the debts from World War I made it infeasible. Even the winners in World War I tried to back all the paper (that the economy had actually run on since the late 1600s) with gold until the 1930s. But they suffered manic booms and devastating busts, over and over, because there was too much economic activity for the gold on hand.

It took until the Great Depression for governments to accept that managing the money supply – injecting money every now and then, managing interest rates, requiring banks to be backed – was not optional, and that they just couldn't do that on gold. Countries recovered from the Great Depression pretty much as they left the rigid gold standard behind, because managing your money supply works much better and is much more stable. A version of the gold standard lingered in the form of the Bretton Woods system until 1971, but rigid backing of currency with gold had been delivered the fatal blow by World War I and then the Great Depression.

But a standard mode of pseudoscience is to adopt and fervently defend a discarded idea, and "gold bugs" were no exception, ardently pushing the version of the gold standard that had just been demonstrated utterly inadequate to a functioning economy.

(Gold bugs are frankly bizarre. There are lots of rarer metals than gold, but you never hear about "rhodium bugs" or "scandium bugs" or even "platinum bugs.")

The John Birch Society is an American far-right fringe group that has long claimed that inflation comes from central bank increase of the money supply – in fact, they try to redefine "inflation" to mean this – for the purpose of stealing "value" from the people, and that this is why the gold standard was abolished and the Federal Reserve founded.[13] Eustace Mullins furthered these ideas amongst conspiracy theorists with the 1993 reprint of his 1952 book *Secrets of the Federal Reserve*, in which he blames the Fed's creation on "the Rothschild-controlled Bank of England." (Mullins was also famous for his anti-Semitism; every time Mullins said "banker" he meant "Jew," but this mostly isn't *consciously* the case amongst Bitcoiners, who only *occasionally* rant about Zionists.)

These ideas had also been propagated in the mainstream by Ron Paul in the wake of the 2008 credit crunch and the quantitative easing (just printing money, to kick-start the economy) that followed. Though Paul isn't a fan of Bitcoin – he wants a return to actual gold after he abolishes the Fed.[14]

Old ideologies come back when they fill a present desire and there's an opening for them. So these claims, somewhere between incorrect and nonsensical, showed up full-blown in Bitcoin discussion, proponents straight-facedly repeating earlier conspiracy theories as if this was all actually proper economics. Because if it is, then maybe they'll get rich for free!

In this context, and particularly in Bitcoin discourse, you'll see many words that look like English but are actually specialised conspiracy theory jargon. "Liberty" means only freedom from government; "tyranny" means only government; "force" and "violence" mean only government force and violence; "open societies" is a code word for "free market without regulations"; "freedom" means "free market without regulations" and only that.

Pure commodities – gold and silver – haven't done the job of money well for a few hundred years, and Bitcoin wants to be money but was set up to work like a commodity. Nakamoto put a strict limit on the supply of bitcoins: there will only ever be 21 million BTC. So advocates claim Bitcoin is thus, somehow, sufficiently similar to gold to serve as a "store of value" in the desired manner, even "an Internet of *true* value" (whatever "true" means there). This is despite its extreme volatility making it almost useless as a store of value, and despite it being way harder to use as money than any currency should be, even for its few use cases.

Bitcoin ideology bought into the entire Federal Reserve conspiracy package. The Fed is a plot to use inflation to steal value from the people and hand it to a shadowy cabal of elites who also control the government; the worldwide economy is in danger of collapse at any moment due to central banking and fractional reserve banking; gold – sorry, Bitcoin – has intrinsic value that will protect you from this collapse. Advocates repackage and propagate these ideas almost verbatim, even when they almost certainly don't know who or where they trace back to.

Conventional economics views inflation – a decline in money's purchasing power – as a phenomenon of consumer prices, consumer confidence, productivity, commodity and asset prices, etc., which a central bank then responds to with monetary policy. Printing more money *can* cause inflation, but it's not the usual cause. The conspiracy theorist view is that it's the central bank intervention *causing* the inflation. Bitcoin ideology assumes that inflation is a purely monetary phenomenon that can *only* be caused by printing more money, and that Bitcoin is immune due to its strictly limited supply. This was demonstrated trivially false when the price of a bitcoin dropped from $1000 in late 2013 to $200 in early 2015 – 400% inflation – while supply only went up 10%.

Nakamoto's 2008 white paper alluded to these ideas, but the 2009 release announcement for Bitcoin 0.1 states them outright:[15]

> The root problem with conventional currency is all the trust that's required to make it work. The central bank must be trusted not to debase the currency, but the history of fiat currencies is full of breaches of that trust. Banks must be trusted to hold our money and transfer it electronically, but they lend it out in waves of credit bubbles with barely a fraction in reserve. We have to trust them with our privacy, trust them not to let identity thieves drain our accounts. Their massive overhead costs make micropayments impossible.

Bitcoin failed at every one of Nakamoto's aspirations here. The price is ridiculously volatile and has had multiple bubbles; the unregulated exchanges (with no central bank backing) front-run their customers, paint the tape to manipulate the price, and are hacked or just steal their users' funds; and transaction fees and the unreliability of transactions make micropayments completely unfeasible. Because all of this is based in crank ideas that don't work.

A week after Bitcoin 0.1 was released, Jonathan Thornburg wrote on the Cryptography and Cryptography Policy mailing list: "To me, this means that no major government is likely to allow Bitcoin in its present form to operate on a large scale."[16] In practice, governments totally did, and treated it like any other financial innovation: give it room to run, make it very clear that regulation still applies, give it a bit more room to run, repeat. The advocates' ideas of how governments work were already at odds with completely predictable reality.

(I'm still baffled at the notion that the governments of first-world countries are somehow *fundamentally against* the idea of people doing well with innovations in finance.)

## Austrian economics

The acceptable face of this conspiracy cluster is Austrian economics, first put together in its present form by Ludwig von Mises (hence "Austrian"). Its key technique is *praxeology*, in which economic predictions are made *entirely* by extrapolating from fundamental axioms. It explicitly repudiates any sort of empirical testing of predictions, and holds that you can't predict future behaviour from past behaviour even in principle, so testing your claims is meaningless:[17]

> The subject matter of all historical sciences is the past. They cannot teach us anything which would be valid for all human actions, that is, for the future too …
>
> No laboratory experiments can be performed with regard to human action. We are never in a position to observe the change in one element only, all other conditions of the event remaining unchanged. Historical experience as an experience of complex phenomena does not provide us with facts in the sense in which the natural sciences employ this term to signify isolated events tested in experiments. The information conveyed by historical experience cannot be used as building material for the construction of theories and the prediction of future events …

> [Praxeology's] statements and propositions are not derived from experience. They are, like those of logic and mathematics, a priori. They are not subject to verification or falsification on the ground of experience and facts.

Despite this, proponents keep *making* predictions and claims, and insisting they are, somehow, still worth listening to and applying to the world.

Austrian economics was heavily promoted by heterodox[*] economist Murray Rothbard, founder of the Ludwig von Mises Institute. Rothbard invented the term *anarcho-capitalism* for his ideology that a complete absence of government is essential, and that property rights, which are paramount, will somehow still function without it. An offence against one's property is equivalent to an offence against the self; so the "Non-Aggression Principle" holds that trespassing is aggression, but the owner shooting you for trespassing somehow isn't. Police will be replaced with private security services and courts with arbitration services. Really extreme Austrians like Hans-Herman Hoppe admit that all this would lead directly to functional feudalism. Which becomes neoreaction and the alt-right, but Elizabeth Sandifer already wrote that book.[18] [†]

Austrian economics has produced vast quantities of detailed theory to support the claim that a gold standard is the only sensible way to run an economy – rather than the more conventional view that a zero-sum economy quickly seizes up, both in theory and practice[‡] – and that central banks and fractional reserve banking will inexorably lead to a collapse. *Disaster is imminent*, and you need to be hoarding *gold*.

Sadly for Bitcoin, most Austrian economists aren't fans – even as Bitcoiners remain huge fans of Austrian economics.[19] You will find Austrian jargon in common use in the cryptocurrency world.

Proponents of Austrian economics include the fringe economics blog *Zero Hedge*, which has confidently predicted two hundred of the last two recessions. *Zero Hedge* covers Bitcoin extensively, and Bitcoiners are fans in turn.

---

[*] *Heterodox*: a crank with a job. Austrian economics is funded by rich people who want theoretical backing for being selfish.

[†] I'd never encountered American-style ideological libertarianism and anarcho-capitalism before the Internet. When I first heard about it, I honestly thought it was a wacky Swiftian political satire that nobody could actually *believe*.

[‡] Austrian economists *really hate* the example of (see Wikipedia) the Capitol Hill Babysitting Co-op.

# Chapter 3: The incredible promises of Bitcoin!

Nobody buys a toothbrush on the basis that the toothbrush market will go *to the moon!* (There hasn't so far been a toothbrush asset bubble.) This is, however, the standard selling point for cryptocurrencies. As is claiming the selling point is anything other than hope that it will go to the moon.

Advocates claim all manner of practical use cases for Bitcoin. A lot of the claims contradict each other, and indeed the actual software; others merely run aground on reality. They mix up hypothetical ideas (most of it) and what is robust technology that actually exists (almost none), with bogus economics to boot. Just as long as they can get you to *buy Bitcoin.*

After the first Bitcoin bubble popped, many of these claims were carried forward unaltered into contemporary business "Blockchain" hype.

The Bitcoin Wiki answers many common objections on a "Myths" page.[20] The answers are of varying persuasiveness.

## Decentralised! Secured by math!

Bitcoiners hold that immunity to central control is so overwhelmingly important that it's completely worth all that electricity wasted on mining. And the maths is unbreakable!

In practice, mining naturally recentralises due to economies of scale, so a few large mining pools now control transaction processing – and even though the cryptography is mathematically robust, the rest of the system is approximate, with attacks being a matter of how much economic power you can bring to bear. Pools with a large percentage of the mining power can attack the system in various ways, and have been caught doing so in the past. (*See* Chapter 5: How Bitcoin mining centralised.)

And that's before even considering bad user security, or exchanges written in dodgy PHP. Bitcoin's cryptography is solid, but it's a bit like putting a six inch thick steel vault door in a cardboard frame.

## Anonymous!

Bitcoin was widely touted early on as anonymous – on the blockchain, nobody knows you're a dog. Of course, with every confirmed transaction logged in the blockchain forever, it's pseudonymous at best; as the case of Ross Ulbricht and the Silk Road showed (*see* Chapter 4), law enforcement will happily do the tedious legwork of tracing your transactions if you motivate them sufficiently.

There are ways to increase your anonymity, such as *mixers* – send coins to an address, they shuffle them with other people's coins, and you get them back later minus a percentage. (Assuming the mixer isn't a scam that just takes your coins.) There is also the trick of buying a chain of other cryptocurrencies in succession, to cloud your trail over multiple chains; though exchanges are increasingly wise to this one and tend to kick such traders off for obvious money laundering.

## Instant! No fees!

Nakamoto's original 2008 white paper notes that Bitcoin will naturally progress to a transaction fee-based economy to pay the miners. "No fees!" was still a perennial claim for many years, until mid-2015 when it became glaringly obvious that this simply didn't hold any more.

Blocks in the blockchain were limited to 1 megabyte early on. But the blocks are now full – Bitcoin has reached capacity. This means a transaction may fail or be delayed for hours or days (if it isn't just dropped), unless the user correctly guesses a large enough fee to get their transaction into the block. The Bitcoin community is unable to agree on how to fix this.

The fees and delays mean that Nakamoto's 2009 dream of Bitcoin as a channel for micropayments becomes impossible (even as that dream contradicts the 2008 white paper).

## No chargebacks!

Transactions are irreversible, and no human can intervene to fix mistakes. You might think this is obviously bad, but the white paper claims this as an *advantage* of the Bitcoin system. Bitcoin advocates fervently believe that the one thing merchants fear most is credit card chargebacks, and that "no chargebacks" is the best hook Bitcoin could have.

Bitcoin Wiki's "Myths" page says: "Allowing chargebacks implies that it is possible for another entity to take your money from you. You can have either total ownership rights of your money, or fraud protection, but not both."

In practice, consumers, businesses and banks overwhelmingly expect errors or thefts to be reversible. There is negligible demand for a system where human intervention to reverse an error is impossible. Even merchants, as much as they dislike chargebacks, turn out to prefer consumer confidence and payment methods people will actually use.

When mining rig manufacturer Butterfly Labs failed to deliver rigs on time, credit card and PayPal purchasers could do (and did) chargebacks; those who bought using bitcoins were out of luck.

(Butterfly Labs also bought satirical site buttcoin.org to replace a detailed takedown of one of their terrible mining offerings with an advertising page;[21] the main product of this effort was the Federal Trade Commission saying "buttcoin."[22])

# Be your own bank!

"Secured by math" means the cryptography is strong – but it says nothing about everything else you need to use bitcoins safely in practice. "Be your own bank" means you take on the job of providing *all* the security and technical knowledge that a regulated professional institution normally would.

The Bitcoin Wiki offers a page with step-by-step instructions on how to secure your personal Bitcoin wallet that would dismay even a typical IT professional, let alone a casual computer user.[23] You will need a security specialist's understanding of the possible modes of attack on a modern operating system, how to encrypt all data securely and yet accessibly, password strength, backup procedures, how to securely erase a disk, the quirks of whatever Bitcoin wallet software you're using ...

This is why the vast majority of users store their bitcoins on an exchange like it's an unregulated and uninsured savings bank, even though the exchanges' security and reliability record is dismal. (Keeping your money in a sock under someone else's bed.)

## Better than Visa, PayPal or Western Union!

There is no way on earth that Bitcoin could possibly scale to being a general utility. At 1 megabyte per block, the blockchain can only do a maximum of 7 transactions per second, *worldwide total*. Typical throughput in early 2017 was 2 to 4 TPS.

Compare with the systems Bitcoin claims it can replace: PayPal, which ran about 115 TPS by late 2014;[24] Visa, whose 2015 capacity was 56,000 TPS;[25] even Western Union alone averaged 29 TPS in 2013.[26]

Various off-chain workarounds have been proposed (sidechains, Lightning Network); advocates talk about these as if they already exist, rather than being stuck in development hell.

Advocates sometimes excuse the electricity wasted on mining by claiming that it's nothing compared to the energy used by the conventional banking system; this is simply false, with Bitcoin mining taking thousands of times the energy per transaction.[27]

## Remittances!

Bitcoin is put forward as the obvious replacement for Western Union for people working in rich countries to send money back to their families in poor ones – even for the present-day case where you need to convert to and from bitcoins at each end.

The bit where you transmit money between countries is not expensive at all – you pay Western Union to maintain services, cash on hand and so on for the "last mile" of the journey. With Bitcoin, the conversion fees at each end usually add up to more than the banking network would charge; the ten-minute transmission time (if it's that fast) turns out not to make up for the delays in purchasing the coins for the sender or selling them for the receiver; the price volatility is extreme enough to affect the amount transmitted. The remittance case could only work if Bitcoin were already a generally accepted international currency.

Rebit.ph is making a serious attempt at Bitcoin-based remittances to the Philippines, but has foundered on the volatility of Bitcoin prices and difficulties in exchanging the bitcoins for pesos at the far end. They eventually had to set up a Bitcoin exchange just to have sufficient conventional currency on hand.[28]

## Bank the unbanked!

There are over two billion people in the world who have no bank account or access to even basic financial services; "banking the unbanked" is much discussed in international development circles. Around 2013, Bitcoin advocates started claiming that Bitcoin could help with this problem. Unfortunately:

- The actual problems that leave people unbanked are the bank being too far away, or bureaucratic barriers to setting up an account when you get there.

- Unless they use an exchange (which would functionally be a bank), they'd need an expensive computer and a reliable Internet connection to hold and update 120 gigabytes of blockchain.

- Bitcoin is way too volatile to be a reliable store of value.

- How do they convert it into local money they can spend?

- 7 transactions per second worldwide total means Bitcoin couldn't cope with just the banked, let alone the unbanked as well.

- A centralised service similar to M-Pesa (a very popular Kenyan money transfer and finance service for mobile phones) might work, but M-Pesa exists, works and is trusted by its users – and goes a long way toward solving the problems with access to banking that Bitcoin claims to.

Advocates will nevertheless say "but what about the unbanked?" as if Bitcoin is an obvious slam-dunk answer to the problem and nothing else needs to be said. But no viable mechanism to achieve this has ever been put forward.

# Economic equality!

Bitcoin offered "equality" in that anyone could mine it. But in practice, Bitcoin was substantially mined early on – early adopters have *most* of the coins. The design was such that early users would get vastly better rewards than later users for the same effort.

Cashing in these early coins involves pumping up the price and then selling to later adopters, particularly during the bubbles. Thus, Bitcoin was not a Ponzi or pyramid scheme, but a pump-and-dump. Anyone who bought in after the earliest days is functionally the sucker in the relationship.

"Why should I spend money to make these guys rich?" is such a common objection that the Bitcoin Wiki answered it: "Early adopters are rewarded for taking the higher risk with their time and money." It is entirely unclear what the "risk" involved was, or how this would convince anyone who didn't already agree.

In economics, the *Gini coefficient* is the standard measure of how inequitable a society is. This is tricky to determine for Bitcoin, as it's not quite a "society" in the Gini sense, one person may have multiple addresses and many addresses have been used only once or a few times. (The commonly-cited figure of 0.88 is based on one small exchange in 2011.[29]) However, a Citigroup analysis from early 2014 notes: "47 individuals hold about 30 percent, another 900 hold a further 20 percent, the next 10,000 about 25% and another million about 20%"; and the distribution "looks much like the distribution of wealth in North Korea and makes China's and even the US' wealth distribution look like that of a workers' paradise."[30]

Dorit Ron and Adi Shamir found in a 2012 study that only 22% of then-existing bitcoins were in circulation at all, there were a total of 75 active users or businesses with any kind of volume, one (unidentified) user owned a quarter of all bitcoins in existence, and one large owner was trying to hide their pile by moving it around in thousands of smaller transactions.[31]

(Shamir is one of the most renowned cryptographers in the world and the "S" in "RSA encryption"; of course, Bitcoiners attempted to disparage his credentials and abilities.)

The usual excuse is to say that it's still early days for Bitcoin. However, there are no forces that would correct the imbalance.

# The supply is limited! The price can only go up!

Bitcoin is an imitation of the gold standard; the supply is strictly limited. Advocates tout this as an advantage as a currency. Hal Finney said in 2009:[32]

> As an amusing thought experiment, imagine that Bitcoin is successful and becomes the dominant payment system in use throughout the world. Then the total value of the currency should be equal to the total value of all the wealth in the world.

Bitcoin advocates then adopted this idle musing as something that would *obviously* happen.

The problem is that Bitcoin is deflationary. Let's assume for a moment that Bitcoin economic theories work. As economic value traded in Bitcoins increases, the limited supply means the economic value per bitcoin goes up, which means that the price of things in bitcoins goes down. This means the dollar value of one bitcoin indeed goes up! However, it also means there's absolutely no incentive to spend your bitcoins if they'll always be worth more tomorrow. This means economic activity goes down, and if there are alternatives – other cryptocurrencies, or just using existing payment systems – Bitcoin loses users and interest.

In practice, the price of Bitcoin goes up when there is demand for it as a speculative commodity, drops when demand drops and is hugely volatile because trading is so thin. But it's important to note that this idea wouldn't work even in hypothetical Bitcoin economics.

# But Bitcoin saved Venezuela!

Periodically, there will be a rash of news stories claiming that Bitcoin has become popular in some country suffering economic problems, such as Venezuela, India or Argentina – because the word "Bitcoin" makes a headline catchy, even if there's nothing to the story. This transmutes into claims that Bitcoin will definitely take over the world, any day now. Or advocates will respond to scepticism "but Venezuela!"

These claims always fall apart on closer examination. Venezuela is a typical example: all the coverage traces back to a story in Libertarian magazine *Reason*, fiercely advocating Bitcoin as a way to avert the spectres of socialism and regulation.[33] One of their interviewees had been arrested for stealing electricity to mine bitcoins, which the author describes as a "government crackdown" on "freedom" because "bitcoin mining is arguably the best possible use of electricity in Venezuela".

A story in *The Guardian* in the wake of the *Reason* story appears to be where the rest of the press picked it up. It speaks of some Venezuelans relying on Bitcoin for "basic necessities," and was based on interviews with a Bitcoin exchange owner, one of his employees and two of his customers.[34] The author had previously written of Argentina and bitcoin.[35]

These two questionably-founded stories were echoed and elaborated upon by the rest of the press, including – among *many* others – the *Washington Post* claiming that Bitcoin mining is "big business" in Venezuela,[36] the *New York Times* that Bitcoin has "gained prominence" *because* of Venezuela[37] or BBC News repeating claims from a Bitcoin boosterism blog[38] – all of this being factoids repeated in a media game of "telephone."

The Venezuelan volume on LocalBitcoins (a site for arranging person-to-person Bitcoin trades) at the time was on the order of 200-300 BTC per week,[39] which isn't nothing, but is negligible in the context of a whole country, and has tracked fairly closely with LocalBitcoins usage in other countries.

## When the economy collapses, Bitcoin will save you!

No, really: there are Bitcoin advocates who seriously look forward to economic collapse as an opportunity for Bitcoin – continued availability of high powered computing machinery, mining chip foundries, fast Internet and electricity presumably being absolutely assured in the grim meathook Mad Max petrolpunk future. (And we can use colloidal Litecoin for antibiotics.*)

Even lesser crises get them all excited. Nick Szabo wrote up how to fix the Greek financial crisis of 2015 with Bitcoin.[40] Someone responded to the Cyprus financial crisis of 2013 (which did include the much-feared government haircut of bank account deposits over

---

\* "The silver to Bitcoin's gold"… oh, never mind.

the insured €100,000) with a house music anthem about "the blockchain."[41]

## You can use Bitcoin to buy drugs on the Internet!

This one is completely true and accurate, but Bitcoin advocates don't seem to like mentioning it for some reason.

# Chapter 4: Early Bitcoin: the rise to the first bubble

## The tulip bulb era

Asset bubbles follow a standard progression:

1. *Stealth phase:* The price of an asset is going up.
2. *Awareness phase:* Some investors become confident, enthused by the rise.
3. *Mania phase:* Popular buzz; media coverage. The public see these first investors and buy because others are buying, with the implicit assumption that there will always be Greater Fools to sell it on to. This is what makes a bubble: investing to sell to other investors. Someone will say that the old rules don't apply any more.
4. *Blowoff phase:* The old rules turn out to still apply. The bubble runs out of Greater Fools; prices collapse.

The asset need not be a commodity, *e.g.*, the Beanie Baby craze of the late 1990s, in which the asset was various instances of a manufactured product line controlled by a single company. (Though after that crash, at least you had a nice cuddly toy.) The key point is the "mania phase."

Charles Mackay's superlative *Memoirs of Extraordinary Popular Delusions and the Madness of Crowds*, first published in 1841, remains an excellent and accessible introduction to economic bubbles and the thinking behind them, starting with the Tulip Mania of 1637 and the South Sea Bubble of 1720.[42] Bitcoin is a completely standard example.

The first bitcoin was mined in January 2009, but for the first year the enthusiasts just exchanged them amongst themselves for fun. The first known conversion to conventional currency was by Martti Malmi, ardent anarcho-capitalist and Bitcoin core coder: "I sold 5,050 BTC for $5,02 on 2009-10-12."[43] The first exchange site was bitcoinmarket.com, which opened 6 February 2010. The famous first commercial transaction (two pizzas, cost $30 including tip, for 10,000 BTC[44]) was a few months later, on 22 May 2010.[45]

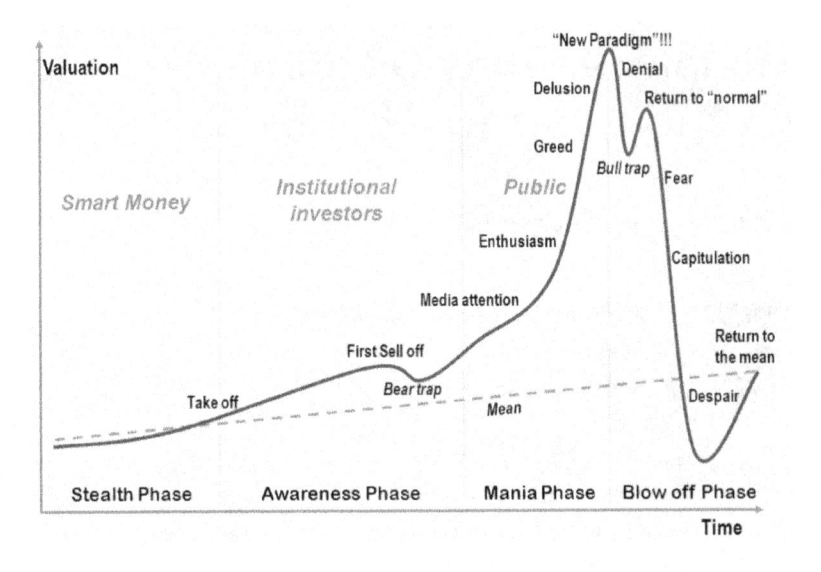

*"Stages in a bubble" by Jean-Paul Rodrigue, 2008.*[46]

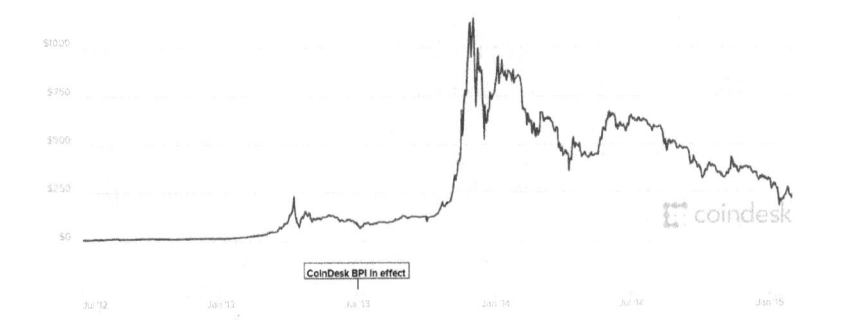

*Bitcoin prices, January 2012 to January 2015. Totally no resemblance to the above.*
*Data: coindesk.com*

From there the price rose steadily to 1c in July 2010. Bitcoin version 0.3 was mentioned on 11 July by tech news site Slashdot, gaining it some notice in the technology world, and inspiring the founding of the Mt. Gox exchange. In November 2010, WikiLeaks released the US diplomatic cables dump; the site was cut off from Visa, Mastercard and PayPal shortly after at the behest of the US government, but could still receive donations in Bitcoin. The price of a bitcoin hit $1 by February 2011.

In April 2011, anarcho-capitalist and businessman Roger Ver, who had made his fortune with computer parts business Memory Dealers, heard a segment about Bitcoin on the libertarian podcast Free Talk Live. Ver promptly went to Mt. Gox, the Bitcoin exchange mentioned on the show, and bought $25,000 worth of Bitcoins, single-handedly pushing the price up from $1.89 to $3.30 over the next few days. He would spend the next few years buying and advocating Bitcoin, branding himself "Bitcoin Jesus."

The earliest minor bubble grew and popped in June 2011, after an article on the Silk Road darknet market, mentioning Bitcoin, in *Gawker*. 1 BTC momentarily peaked at $30, before dropping to $15 after Mt. Gox was hacked in June, and slowly declining to $2 by December. By a year later, in December 2012, it had risen to $13. (With minor wobbles such as the August 2012 crash when the Pirateat40 Ponzi scheme collapsed.)

In this era, Bitcoin was largely evangelised by advocates for its hypothetical use cases and political possibilities. The actual use case was buying drugs on the Silk Road, the first notable darknet market, which started in January 2011. Mining at home could still be profitable at this time.

The bubble really got going in early 2013. By March, the price had hit $50 and *The Economist* warned that this was really obviously a bubble, noting how closely the price tracked Google searches for "bitcoin".[47] It hit $266 in April after a month of going up 5-10% *daily*, crashed to $130 in May and $100 in June, and rose steadily through the rest of the year – with occasional hiccups when Mt. Gox, by now the largest Bitcoin exchange, handling 70% of all Bitcoin transactions, had unexpected delays in allowing customers to cash out in US dollars.

The Silk Road was busted in early October and Bitcoin plummeted from $145 to $110. But it rose again with increased interest from China, with highly efficient mining operations starting up with custom-made ASIC mining chips, and local exchanges gaining great popularity.[48] The price started November at $350, and peaked at $1250 – or at least that was the spot price on Mt. Gox, and users were once again reporting problems withdrawing dollars. In December it started at $500, jumped to $1000 and fell back to $650 – the standard bubble peak had passed.

Mt. Gox stumbled along for a few months then finally collapsed, taking everyone's deposits with it; it later came out that they had been insolvent since at least 2012. The price declined through the rest of 2014, bottoming out just below $200 in early 2015. As a currency, Bitcoin did somewhat worse in 2014 than the Russian rouble and the Ukrainian hryvnia.

It is important to note that Bitcoin advocates believed the late 2013 peak was not a bubble, but the natural upward progression of the price as Bitcoin increased its share of the economy; *e.g.*, Rick Falkvinge's March 2013 piece "The Target Value for Bitcoin Is Not Some $50 or $100: It is $100,000 to $1,000,000."[49] The collapse came as a complete shock to many; when Mt. Gox went down, Reddit /r/bitcoin posted and pinned suicide hotline numbers.

# The art of the steal

As a financial instrument born without regulation, Bitcoin quickly turned into an iterative exploration of precisely why each financial regulation exists. A "trustless" system attracts the sort of people who just can't be trusted.

Many crypto scams are quite complex; some are simpler than you might expect. Many are everyday dodgy investment opportunities but with Bitcoin. It can be difficult to distinguish malice from incompetence. The general problem is that you don't know who or where these people are, and they routinely just disappear with everyone's money.

Scams common to the cryptocurrency world include:[50]

- *Ponzi schemes:* in which early investors are paid using money from later ones. These are so attractive to crypto fans that when Ethereum took blockchains and added "smart contracts" (programs that run on the blockchain), the first thing people did was write automatic "honest" Ponzis.

- *High-yield investment programmes:* a variety of Ponzi scheme. You might think it obvious that no investment scheme could pay 6% interest per week sustainably, particularly when it claims a "secret" investment strategy, but what worked on Bernie Madoff's victims works on Bitcoiners.

- *Coin doublers:* send it a small amount of bitcoins and you'll get double back! (No reason is given why anyone would just double your money.) Send a larger amount straight after and

... you won't. You'd think people would catch on, but years later these keep popping up and finding suckers.

(There's another layer of scam in there: the "doubler" *never* sends back coins. But it's publicised with a "warning" about the scam. Others think "hold on, if I only send coins once it'll never see me as a repeat user!" They send in a small amount of coins, which of course is not doubled. It's a scam which relies on the sucker thinking they're the scammer.[51] A similar scam ran in the game RuneScape.[52])

- *Mining software:* if you aren't designing your own mining chips and running them off super-cheap power, you won't have been able to break even mining Bitcoin since late 2013. But people keep claiming you can still mine on your PC. The software frequently includes malware.

- *Mining hardware:* there are real sellers of mining hardware (though you are unlikely to come out ahead of costs). The scam is to run it for months "testing" it: customers pay for hardware, you use their money to build it and you mine with it for the few months it's viable before you send it to them. Butterfly Labs was the most notorious culprit,[53] but far from the only one. (Butterfly's co-founder turned out to have a conviction for mail fraud;[54] Bitcoin scammers are often serial scammers.)

- *Cloud mining:* you invest in remote mining hardware. Many such schemes appear indistinguishable from Ponzis; there is generally no evidence the money-printing machine you're renting even exists.

- *Scam wallets:* sites offering greater transaction anonymity, but which just take everyone's bitcoins after a while.

- *Biased "provably fair" gambling:* "Provably fair" gambling sites generate their random numbers in advance then send you a cryptographic hash of the sequence of numbers, so you don't know the numbers ahead of time but you can verify the hash afterwards.[55] Some sites, if you *don't* grab the hash, then use a biased sequence of numbers instead.[56]

- *Scam versions of normal services:* exchanges, bitcoin mixers, shopping deal sites and so on. You have no idea who these people are, and every now and then they'll just take your bitcoins or link you to phishing or other scam sites, possibly including the gift of malware.

Fortunately, Bitcointalk.org deals harshly with scammers: it may add a "scammer" tag to someone's forum name, or list their site in the "List of Bitcoin Scam Sites" thread.

Many Bitcoin advocates consider the scammers worth it to be free of government regulation. Anarcho-capitalist Jeffrey Tucker wrote an amazing apologia, "A Theory Of The Scam,"[57] in which he admits Bitcoin is suffused with fraud, but posits that "scam artists are the evil cousins of genuine entrepreneurs" and are actually a sign of *health* for an area – so, since good things had scams, this scam-riddled thing must therefore be good! (With all this horse poop there's *gotta* be a pony in here.) No doubt subprime-mortgage-backed collateral debt obligations, Business Consulting International and Bernard L. Madoff Investment Securities LLC were just severely underpriced investment opportunities.

## Pirateat40: Bitcoin Savings & Trust

> Now that Pirateat40 closed down his operatations thanks to all the fud that was going on and growing on the forum, I expect everyone that spreads this fud, accused and insulted Pirate and the people that supported him to apologize. Not only did Pirate brought us a great opportunity for investors (once in a lifetime actually), he did help stabilise and grow steadily bitcoin price, volume exchange, and thus contributed to the success of bitcoin. For that, Pirate, I want to thank you. You've done a wonderful work, and I hope you're stay around here.
>
> – Raphael Nicolle, founder of the Bitfinex exchange, just after Bitcoin Savings & Trust collapsed[58]

By 2012, as the Bitcoin subculture was heating up, high-yield investment programmes – *i.e.*, Ponzi schemes – had begun manifesting in the bitcointalk.org "Lending" section. One user even literally called high-yield investment programmes a "Bitcoin Killer App".[59]

The most famous of these was Bitcoin Savings & Trust, opened in late 2011 by Trendon Shavers, *a.k.a.* Bitcointalk forum user Pirateat40 (named after the song "A Pirate Looks at Forty" by Jimmy Buffett). It offered interest of 7% weekly – or about 3300% annually – on investments over 25,000 BTC. Hands up anyone who can see a problem here …

Investment was strictly limited and accounts were much-coveted. Pirateat40 was a VIP Donor (50 BTC) to Bitcointalk; he built up a strong forum reputation and got other highly-rated people to resell his investment programme, offering "Pirate Pass-Through" bonds. Those who pointed out that this had all the really obvious signs of being a Ponzi scheme had much lower forum reputations, especially after saying this.

Pirateat40 claimed to be making his money from Bitcoin market arbitrage, including selling bitcoins in person or in large quantities. Others were not reassured; he had so many bitcoins in his scheme that others worried at the effect on Bitcoin itself when the scheme collapsed.[60]

On 17 August 2012, basic arithmetic reasserted itself. Pirateat40 announced the closure of Bitcoin Savings & Trust. He said he had 500,000 BTC (about $5.6 million) in the fund as of its closure and that he would be returning it to investors.[61] Apart from some refunds to friends and long-time investors, this of course didn't happen.

On 17 September, Pirateat40 announced on IRC that "the earliest estimated time that coins can begin moving is Friday, Oct 12th" (not that any coins actually moved on 12 October). He also declared that "Those looking to file a suit against me or BTCST will not be eligible for repayment" and "Threats are taken seriously by myself and my attorney. A few of you will find out how serious I mean."[62]

Burnt investors tracked him down. They found his name, they found where he lived, they even found his business that had closed at the same time. They initially had some trouble convincing the authorities not only that this was really money, but that they had given it to some guy on an Internet forum called "Pirate" on the strength of him saying "sure, I'll double your bitcoins, no worries."

The SEC started investigations and depositions in late 2012. It turned out Shavers didn't have a lawyer after all, and spilled the beans on his entire operation in deposition, including admitting to destroying evidence (server logs) that had specifically been subpoenaed.[63] He did finally find a lawyer, who set up a Bitcoin donation address to fund the case since Shavers' assets had been frozen.[64]

The SEC filed a civil enforcement action against Shavers in July 2013.[65] As well as running the scheme as a Ponzi, he had taken about

150,000 BTC to day trade on Bitcoinica and Mt. Gox, from which he took about $150,000 to spend personally. His lawyer's entire defense was that bitcoins were not "money" under US law because they were not legal tender; the judge didn't buy it, and Shavers was required in September 2014 to pay back $40.7 million.[66] He was also prosecuted for criminal securities fraud for the Ponzi in November 2014,[67] pled guilty in September 2015 and was sentenced to one and a half years in jail.[68] The lawyer later maintained that the SEC only went after Shavers because they were upset they hadn't caught Bernie Madoff in time, and not at all because Shavers stole millions of dollars from people.[69]

The astounding thing is how successful such an obvious Ponzi had been. Pirateat40 held about 7% of all bitcoins in circulation at the time. Some Bitcoiners offered insurance against Bitcoin Savings & Trust failing, then put the insurance premiums into the scheme; or just didn't pay up when it went down. Others offered investment schemes that were pass-throughs to Pirateat40's scheme, while swearing up and down they weren't.

## Bitcoin exchanges: keep your money in a sock under someone else's bed

"Be your own bank" is actually very hard – particularly with "no chargebacks", meaning that in the event of a theft or even a mistake you're completely out of luck – so almost everyone who uses cryptocurrencies keeps their coins on an exchange. Exchanges also let you trade between different cryptocurrencies, crypto assets and conventional currencies, and some even offer short-selling and other margin trading, which are enormously popular.

Bitcoin exchanges were started by amateur enthusiasts. Most were computer programmers whose approach to anything outside their field was "I know PHP, how hard could running an exchange be?" As Dunning and Kruger pointed out in 1999,[*] this approach tends not to work out so well.

In real securities trading, you can presume the exchanges themselves are not going to mess you around, and indeed that they're basically competent. You can't assume either with crypto exchanges.

---

[*]  Wikipedia: Dunning-Kruger effect. From which another name for bitcoins, "Dunning-Krugerrands."

The gateways to the world of real money are stringently regulated – you'll need to give amazing quantities of government ID to these people you know nothing about – but inside the exchanges it's the Wild West.

Hacks, supposed hacks and exchanges just disappearing with all their customers' money remain dismally regular occurrences. As of March 2015, a full third of all Bitcoin exchanges up to then had been hacked, and nearly half had closed.[70] Since the exchanges are largely uninsured, unregulated and not required to keep reserves, depositors' money goes up in smoke.

It's not just scamminess on the part of the proprietors, but sheer jawdropping incompetence:

- Bitomat, then the third-largest exchange, were keeping the whole site's wallet file on an Amazon Web Services EC2 server in the cloud that didn't have separate backups and was set to "ephemeral," *i.e.,* it would disappear if you restarted it. Guess what happened in July 2011? Whoops.[71]

- Bitcoinica was its sixteen-year-old creator's first serious PHP project. He read up on PHP, Ruby on Rails, personal finance and startups, and wrote an exchange.[72] It collapsed in May 2012: "No database backups … Everyone had root."* The exchange's remaining funds were lost in further hacks, after the administrators turned out to be using their (leaked) Mt. Gox password as their LastPass password.[73]

- BitPay claimed to be fully insured. It suffered a "phishing" attack in December 2014, when an attacker broke into an outside partner's computer and sent an email posing as the CFO to the CEO and chairman telling them to send 5,000 BTC to the attacker. The insurer refused to compensate the company, pointing out they had taken out a policy that only covered BitPay computers and physical cash on BitPay's premises, and bitcoins didn't count as physical cash.[74]

- AllCrypt ran their exchange off a MySQL database … and were running WordPress on the same database, and their WordPress got hacked such as to allow access to the

---

* genjix. Comment on "[Emergency ANN] Bitcoinica site is taken offline for security investigation". Bitcointalk.org Bitcoin Forum > Bitcoin > Bitcoin Discussion, 25 May 2012. "root" is the administrator account for a Unix or Linux server.

exchange data.[75] The same thing happened to Bitcoin lending startup Loanbase.[76]

- Cryptsy appeared to collapse from a "hack" in January 2016 with much apology from the proprietor; the court-appointed receiver's report details how the proprietor ran off with all the bitcoins and moved to China to start a new exchange.[77]

- Kraken publicly blamed web content distribution network Cloudflare for its website problems.[78] Cloudflare's CEO went so far as to publicly tweet that Kraken hadn't paid its bill in months. "Let's get the facts straight. Credit card provided for payment expired. After 3 warnings you were downgraded to a free account."[79]

To be fair, conventional banks say "Yes, Mr. Smith, I'm sorry, but it seems we misplaced all your money irretrievably. Yes, yours in particular. It's gone. Forever. No, I'm sorry, but we aren't liable. Have a nice day!" all the time. *No wait, they don't do anything of the sort.* Not since regulation, insurance and central bank backing were put into place.

# The rise and fall of Mt. Gox

I'm Roger Ver, long time Bitcoin advocate and investor. Today I'm at the Mt. Gox world headquarters in Tokyo, Japan. I had a nice chat with Mt. Gox CEO, Mark Karpelès, about their current situation. He showed me multiple bank statements, as well as letters from banks and lawyers. I'm sure that all the current withdrawal problems at Mt. Gox are being caused by the traditional banking system, not because of a lack of liquidity at Mt. Gox. The traditional banking partners that Mt. Gox needs to work with are not able to keep up with the demands of the growing Bitcoin economy. The dozens of people that make up the Mt. Gox team are hard at work establishing additional banking partners, that eventually will make dealing with Mt. Gox easier for all their customers around the world. For now, I hope that everyone will continue working on Bitcoin projects that will help make the world a better place.

– Roger Ver, July 2013, during the first rumblings at Mt. Gox.[80] (He later apologised.[81])

Bitcoin got its first big publicity push with the announcement of version 0.3 on technology news site Slashdot on 11 July 2010.[82] * †

At this time, Jed McCaleb was a programmer at a loose end. He had previously developed eDonkey, an early file sharing network, which was shut down in late 2005 after being sued by the Recording Industry Association of America. He then went on to develop a game, The Far Wilds, leaving that to its community in 2009.

McCaleb saw the Slashdot post, tried and failed to buy some bitcoins, and thought an exchange would be a good idea. (Early Bitcoin core developer Martti Malmi had an exchange site, but it wasn't very usable.[83]) He had run the "Magic: The Gathering Online Exchange," a trading site for an online card game, for a few months in 2007, using the domain name mtgox.com; he quickly wrote some exchange software in PHP and reused the name because his girlfriend liked it.

McCaleb announced the site on 17 July and it was an immediate hit, because people could buy and sell bitcoins via PayPal – using his personal account. Furthermore, users could keep both dollars and bitcoins there on the exchange to trade more quickly.

By late 2010, McCaleb was doing well from Mt. Gox, even though it was a completely amateur operation – he didn't even talk to a lawyer about the regulatory implications of his business until December 2010, though it was taking and holding people's actual money, uninsured, unregistered and unregulated. But he was finding it enough work to be annoying, he was tiring of attempted hacker attacks, PayPal kept cutting him off, and he worried about the amounts of money he was personally moving around.

He befriended Mark Karpelès, a French web developer. Karpelès was a massive fan of Japanese animation – his online handle MagicalTux was a reference to the anime *Sailor Moon* – so had moved to Japan in 2009. (He also left France before a 2010 fraud trial, in which he was sentenced in absentia to a year's jail.[84]) McCaleb first offered to sell Mt. Gox to Karpelès in January 2011 and finalised the sale in February, announcing it to the world in March.

---

\* This section draws from *Digital Gold: Bitcoin and the Inside Story of the Misfits and Millionaires Trying to Reinvent Money* by Nathaniel Popper (Harper, 2014). Mark Karpelès has disputed parts of the book's account of events: "Restoring the truth". Blog post, 29 May 2015.

† Disclosure: Mark Karpelès bought me a month of Reddit Gold (value $5) after I posted an early draft of the Bitfinex section of this book to /r/buttcoin, with the note "reddit gold for comedy gold, fair trade I'd say".

The deal used a contract they worked out between them, without either of them using a lawyer. It included terms such as:[85]

> the Seller is uncertain if mtgox.com is compliant or not with any applicable U.S. code or statute, or law of any country.
>
> The buyer agrees to indemnify Seller against any legal action that is taken against Buyer or Seller with regards to mtgox.com or anything acquired under this agreement.

It was only in April, after the handover, that Karpelès realised that 80,000 bitcoins (then worth $62,400) had already been missing when he bought Mt. Gox. McCaleb told him "maybe you don't really need to worry about it" and suggested he buy up more BTC to cover the shortfall, shuffle his internal accounts around, get an investor or just mine more himself – but didn't offer any explanation of where the coins might have got to or how.

Karpelès tried to fill the hole himself, but the price of bitcoins kept going up. By June, the missing coins were worth $800,000. Unfortunately, a nondisclosure agreement with McCaleb meant he felt he couldn't tell anyone about the massive hole in the accounts. (He didn't even reveal it to Mt. Gox's own accountant until shortly before the company went bankrupt in February 2014.)

On 18 and 19 June 2011, someone hacked into Mt. Gox. The attacker shuffled hundreds of thousands of bitcoins around – only inside the exchange, not on the public blockchain, though Mt. Gox was the main trading venue to such a degree that this momentarily drove the price of one BTC from $17 down to 1 cent. (The usual surmise is that the hacker wanted to get as many coins as possible out past Mt. Gox's $1000/day withdrawal limit.) The price oscillated between $1 and $20 for the rest of the day; this severe volatility affected other exchanges.

Around 19:15 UTC on 17 June, someone posted a complete list of 61,016 Mt. Gox usernames, email addresses and password hashes to the Bitcoin forums. Many of the passwords were "unsalted"* and so could be more easily cracked. The attacker appeared to have come in through McCaleb's administrative account, which was still active.

Karpelès went into a panic, taking much of the exchange's Bitcoin store and putting it into offline cold wallets – keys printed on paper and stored in safety deposit boxes around Tokyo – where it couldn't be hacked. Since the hacker's trading was internal to Mt. Gox,

---

\* In cryptography, "salting" is used to make it even harder to work out a password from its hash. Wikipedia: Salt (cryptography).

Karpelès was able to roll back most of the transactions; eventual losses were a few thousand BTC, which the company could cover.

Roger Ver, who was also living in Japan by then, came over to help Mt. Gox (still a one-man operation at this stage) in dealing with the hack, and got to know Karpelès – Ver realised that Mt. Gox was critical at this time to Bitcoin's continued growth.

In the aftermath of the hack, Karpelès' paranoia overcame accounting considerations. He kept putting off reconciling the cold wallets with customer accounts, even as his accountant begged him to, as taking them out of cold storage would risk them being hackable. Thus, Mt. Gox was increasingly running on virtual paper money that it wasn't keeping track of.

Mt. Gox continued in this manner through 2012 and 2013. Karpelès took on staff, but remained chronically unable to manage or delegate to them. Ver sometimes had to visit the Mt. Gox offices to make sure his own important transactions went through. The company was still by far the largest Bitcoin exchange, running on the increasing popularity of the Silk Road, as it struggled to keep up with demand – 75,000 new users joined in the first ten days of April 2013.

On 14 May 2013, the US government seized $2.9 million from Mt. Gox, shutting down the main account it used to pay US customers, on the basis that Mt. Gox was transmitting money while having claimed not to be in the money transmission business. In June, the US seized another $2.1 million; Mt. Gox temporarily suspended US dollar transfers. In July, Roger Ver recorded his video assurance that all Mt. Gox's problems were with the "traditional banking system." The exchange partnered with CoinLab to serve its US customers, but this arrangement broke down soon after, Mt. Gox and CoinLab suing each other. By late 2013, customers were complaining of long delays in withdrawing US dollars, just as the Bitcoin bubble was reaching its peak.

On 7 February 2014, Mt. Gox shut down all withdrawals, of bitcoins as well as dollars. According to a leaked "Crisis Strategy Document", Mt. Gox was insolvent after losing track of 744,408 bitcoins – about $350 million at the time.[86] Karpelès had also been topping up the active online hot wallet with coins moved from the paper cold wallets and had not properly kept track.

The bitcoin leak was attributed by Karpelès to what became known as the transaction malleability bug. Bitcoin transaction IDs are not fixed – you can sometimes intercept an unprocessed transaction,

48

modify the transaction ID (though not the amounts or the sender or receiver addresses) and send it on, meaning it's added to the blockchain with a different transaction ID to the one it was sent with. This can lead to someone thinking a transaction they knew they sent didn't go through when it did, and sending the amount again.[87] Once this came out, other exchanges were also attacked in this manner. This news alone crashed the bitcoin price from $700 to $600.[88] (Researchers later ascertained from examining the blockchain that there was no way all of Mt. Gox's claimed 750,000 BTC loss could have been due to transaction malleability attacks.[89])

Mt. Gox had leaked bitcoins before this. In October 2011, 2,609 BTC had been lost to a programming error that sent bitcoins to a nonexistent address.[90] The exchange had been technically insolvent since about 2012, knowingly or unknowingly.[91] It remains entirely unclear how much in total was hacked and how much was just lost.

On 24 February, Mt. Gox finally closed down. $400 million in customer dollars and bitcoins had gone up in smoke.

Karpelès is still dealing with the Japanese authorities, including being arrested for embezzlement in August 2015 and held in custody for several months, with his trial starting in July 2017 (though he maintains his innocence). McCaleb went on to develop the cryptocurrencies Ripple and Stellar; his LinkedIn page details his career back to eDonkey, but chooses to omit Mt. Gox.

# Drugs and the Darknet: The Silk Road

> Both Anne Frank, and Ross Ulbricht created dark markets to help people hide from violent oppressors who were trying to hurt peaceful people.
>
> – Roger Ver[92]

Anonymous or pseudonymous cryptocurrency has one obvious application: paying for things you'd rather not be caught buying or selling. Drug users take to new communication channels as soon as they're invented; the first known e-commerce was the sale of marijuana between Stanford and MIT students over email in 1971 or 1972.[93] Nakamoto noted in September 2010:[94]

> Bitcoin would be convenient for people who don't have a credit card or don't want to use the cards they have, either

don't want the spouse to see it on the bill or don't trust giving their number to "porn guys", or afraid of recurring billing.

Ross Ulbricht grew up in Austin, Texas, born to a well-off family. He was an Eagle Scout; friends and acquaintances were widely impressed by what a polite, helpful young man he was. He studied physics and materials science at college. At Penn State, he took up with the College Libertarians group, and was an activist in support of Ron Paul's 2008 presidential bid.

He left Penn State in 2010 and posted on his LinkedIn page that he was moving from physics to "use economic theory as a means to abolish the use of coercion and aggression amongst mankind ... I am creating an economic simulation to give people a first-hand experience of what it would be like to live in a world without the systemic use of force."

Tor is a protocol and network created in 2002 to let you browse the web in privacy, heavily sponsored by the US government, both for their own use and to aid dissidents in oppressive countries.[95] [96] (And, of course, it's popular with annoying Internet trolls.) You can also set up servers, only available through the Tor network, whose real location can't be traced.[97] Ulbricht realised in 2010 that Tor plus Bitcoin meant you could build a secret marketplace to deal in *anything*, licit or illicit. He adopted the name "Dread Pirate Roberts" (from the book and movie *The Princess Bride*) and launched the Silk Road in January 2011.

The Silk Road was avowedly ideological. Ulbricht was a huge fan of von Mises, Rothbard, Austrian economics and anarcho-capitalism, even hosting a libertarian book club on the Silk Road forums. He consistently put forward the Silk Road as being not just a market, but an experiment to reshape the world.

The site was a sort of eBay for illicit goods. The first sale was psychedelic mushrooms Ulbricht had grown himself, though he quickly moved to just taking a percentage on others' transactions. As well as almost any drug, you could buy steroids, forged government identification (but not *private company* identification), medical and lab supplies (build your drug lab without being flagged), hacking tutorials or drug synthesis tutorials. Sellers were pseudonymous, but relied on building up good ratings from customers. Even investigating FBI and DHS agents found it was surprisingly reliable in both delivery and quality.[98]

One thing you *couldn't* buy was child pornography – even crooks have standards, and Ulbricht forbade child pornography as not being victimless. No weapons of mass destruction, no stolen credit card numbers.

The Silk Road was publicised in March 2011 on libertarian podcast Free Talk Live (the episode that got Roger Ver into Bitcoin). By May, the site, as the one place you could actually use Bitcoin, had driven the price of 1 BTC to $10; when the site went down in mid-May for upgrading, the price of a bitcoin dropped.

The site got a massive boost in June from an article in *Gawker* describing it as an anonymous and convenient drug marketplace, providing a link to the site and directing people to Mt. Gox if they wanted to buy bitcoins to spend there.[99] Jeff Garzik, a Bitcoin core developer, explained to *Gawker* that Bitcoin wasn't "anonymous" but pseudonymous at best, given the blockchain had every transaction ever conducted. "Attempting major illicit transactions with bitcoin, given existing statistical analysis techniques deployed in the field by law enforcement, is pretty damned dumb."

Ulbricht emphasised the site's ideological mission to *Gawker*: "The state is the primary source of violence, oppression, theft and all forms of coercion. Stop funding the state with your tax dollars and direct your productive energies into the black market."

By November 2011, Ulbricht was making $30,000 a month in transaction fees. By early 2012, it was still the only functioning marketplace using bitcoins, and for some time it remained the primary driver of the Bitcoin economy.

Ulbricht had big plans for the Silk Road, as a "brand people can come to trust and rely on … Silk Road chat, Silk Road exchange, Silk Road credit union, Silk Road market, Silk Road everything!"

Around the end of 2012, Ulbricht contracted the murder of a Silk Road administrator who had been arrested, and who he believed had stolen bitcoins from him, fearing he would talk to the police and endanger the Silk Road project. When he received photos of the murdered man, he wired payment for the hit. He would order five more hits over the next few months, the last of which included killing the target's three roommates as well.

(In reality, most were faked by law enforcement agents who were out to catch "Roberts," and one by a scammer who successfully bilked Ulbricht of $500,000. His negotiations and payments to procure murder came up in his eventual trial, and are the subject of a separate Grand Jury indictment in Maryland.)

Ulbricht had been doing all his Silk Road work from his main daily laptop. One afternoon in September 2013, he was sitting in a library, using their wi-fi to administer the site, and talking to a friend in the site's online chat. Two apparently-homeless people started arguing loudly behind him; he turned to look, and the slight young woman using the desk opposite snatched his laptop. She was a government agent. So were the homeless people. So was the friend he was chatting to.

The laptop contained the near-complete collection of smoking gun evidence on the Silk Road, gift-wrapped with a little bow on top. It included the list of Silk Road servers and the names Ulbricht had used to rent them, the Silk Road accounting spreadsheets (including the purchase of the laptop), on-site chat logs, the PHP code for the site itself, photo ID for other Silk Road administrators, all the encryption keys for the site, 144,000 bitcoins … and log.txt, Ulbricht's daily diary of his Silk Road activities: building the site, dealing with business issues, ordering hits on people.[*]

"I imagine that someday I may have a story written about my life, and it would be good to have a detailed account of it," he wrote in January 2012.

The DEA had started investigating the Silk Road in late 2011. They had first started looking into Ulbricht himself in July 2013, when they intercepted a package of fake passports and driver's licenses he had ordered on his own site. He had asked questions on a programming forum about using Tor via PHP as user "Altoid," a handle he had used to promote the Silk Road when he had just launched it, and had included his GMail address, which the FBI obtained a search warrant on. The Silk Road server had been traced when its real address leaked; they had found the name "Frosty" for the apparent system administrator, an alias Ulbricht had used with forum accounts linked to his GMail account and in many other places. Multiple FBI agents had befriended him on the site and even become administrators.

Everyone had assumed that "Dread Pirate Roberts" had the most painstaking operational security imaginable. It turned out Ulbricht

---

[*]   *United States v. Ross William Ulbricht*, S1 14 Cr. 68 (KBF), Government Exhibit 241. This file is commonly referred to as "mycrimes.txt," but its actual name was "log.txt". There were also other personal journal files on the laptop.

was protected by nothing more than an impenetrable shield of narcissism, and an apparent belief that he was too smart and virtuous to be caught.

At trial, on charges of money laundering, computer hacking, conspiracy to traffic fraudulent identity documents and conspiracy to traffic narcotics, Ulbricht's defense amounted to digital identity being ambiguous, with unsubstantiated claims that someone else had set him up.

Unfortunately for Ulbricht, the prosecution had a powerful weapon on its side: overwhelming evidence. Not just from the laptop, but also from the Silk Road server, seized from its hosting company in Iceland. They also had evidence from the Bitcoin blockchain – which, of course, contained a tamper-proofed record of every transaction ever conducted on it and which addresses were involved.[100] Which is why Bitcoin is otherwise known as "prosecution futures".[101]

The defence threw various Hail Mary passes – when your client's been live-logging his criminal activities in real time, there's a limit to what sweet reason and even the most silver tongue can achieve. They admitted Ulbricht had started the Silk Road – then they claimed he then sold it to someone else, who duped him into buying it back just as the FBI was closing in; they claimed that Mark Karpelès was the real "Dread Pirate Roberts" (the DEA had looked into Karpelès in 2012, but decided it wasn't him); they attempted to call surprise last-second expert witnesses (this being slapped down in no uncertain terms by the judge, who told them to stop playing silly buggers[102]); they claimed that all the chat logs, spreadsheets and the daily diary could have somehow been planted on the laptop via BitTorrent; they claimed there was *no way* the real "Dread Pirate Roberts" would be so *stupid* as to have kept a *diary of crimes* on the laptop he *daily ran the site* from.

The charges of procuring murder were lined up to be dealt with in Maryland. However, the negotiations and payments for the hits were brought into the New York trial as evidence for the conspiracy charges, and mentioned in sentencing concerning Ulbricht's character: his freedom-loving anarcho-capitalist ideals and adherence to the non-aggression principle apparently being completely compatible with murdering all the roommates of someone who'd trespassed upon his bitcoins.

In fairness, some of the case against Ulbricht was not flawlessly kosher. The FBI may not have touched all legal bases when tracing the Silk Road server[103] (though the defence failed to challenge the evidence, despite the judge suggesting it to them repeatedly); and two of the agents on the case, Carl Mark Force IV and Shaun Bridges, turned out to have been stealing bitcoins from Ulbricht and the Silk Road and were later jailed. (They too were substantially busted by evidence straight from the blockchain.) Despite this, the evidence was sufficiently convincing that the jury took four hours, including lunch, to find Ulbricht guilty on all seven counts. He was sentenced to life imprisonment without parole.

Ulbricht's fans and family remain unshakably convinced of his innocence and virtuous character: he didn't do it, you can't prove he did it, what he did was harm reduction in the war on drugs, he was jailed just for *running a website* like anyone could, the murders didn't *actually* happen so paying to murder people and all their roommates isn't a crime and shouldn't have been mentioned in the other trial, he hasn't been *convicted* of procuring murder so it probably never happened and he's really a good guy, he was *entrapped* into paying hundreds of thousands of dollars to murder someone and all their roommates, the government ignores the Constitution, also freedom. Darknet posters had threatened the judge, Katherine B. Forrest, and posted private personal information about her in October 2014,[104] and 8chan /baphomet/ posted private information about her again between the verdict and the sentencing.[105] His mother, Lyn Ulbricht, maintains FreeRoss.org:[106]

> They used mostly digital evidence in this trial. Whether or not you believe their evidence … it significantly lowers the standard of evidence at trials. Digital material can be created out of nothing. It doesn't take much imagination to see how this is a threat to us all.

If only the prosecutors had had to hand some sort of cryptographically robust ledger of all transactions, widely distributed, with thousands of verifiable copies available.

Ulbricht's January 2016 appeal was primarily on the basis that the investigation included corrupt law enforcement agents, therefore all the evidence should be thrown out as tainted. This is not an inherently unreasonable basis for an appeal, but, well, log.txt.[107] The appeal was rejected in May 2017, the appeal judges upholding in particular the life sentence without parole on the basis that "Ulbricht was prepared, like other drug kingpins, to protect his profits by paying large sums of money to have individuals who threatened his enterprise murdered".[108]

Silk Road imitators sprang up soon after it started, and many more after it went down. Atlantis ran from March to September 2013. Project Black Flag closed when the Silk Road was busted, stealing all its users' bitcoins. Sheep Marketplace ran from March to December 2013, closing when a vendor apparently stole $100 million in users' bitcoins, though it may have been an exit scam.[109] Silk Road 2.0 started in November 2013, lost bitcoins to the transaction malleability bug, was crippled by arrests, and the operator was finally arrested in November 2014. One undercover federal agent from The Silk Road had been invited to the administrator group of Silk Road 2.0 on its very first day of operation.[110]

# Chapter 5: How Bitcoin mining centralised

## The firetrap era

Bitcoin promised that anyone could mine bitcoins themselves – you could make magical Internet money out of *nothing* (but electricity and hardware). The mining difficulty is adjusted automatically every 14 days to keep the block rate at about one every ten minutes, and in the early days the difficulty was very low indeed.

Mining works by calculating one specific function over and over, as absolutely fast as possible. As far back as 2009, people had realised that graphics cards would be much more efficient[111] – a graphics processing unit (GPU) is designed to run simple calculations very fast to compute video game pixels, and the same sort of processing was able to compute Bitcoin hashes eight hundred times as fast as a general CPU. By 2010, this had become the normal mining method. These were consumer graphics cards, so mining was still accessible to anyone with a few hundred dollars, and it was quite feasible to come out ahead while the price was on the upward slope of the first bubble. (Particularly if you stole the electricity, a popular strategy.)

There are many hilarious and horrifying stories from these days. The now defunct Bitcoin Mining Accidents blog featured home miners' proud photos of their hideously bodged firetrap mining rigs.[112] This famous tale was posted in June 2011:

> I'm done with Bitcoin. It was easy money, but it wasn't worth the (literal) heat.
>
> >had 4 machines with multiple overclocked 5850s in my bedroom
>
> >fan speeds at 100%
>
> >room was warm, but tolerable
>
> >weather suddenly gets hotter one day
>
> >get severe heat stroke while I'm sleeping
>
> >get taken to the ER, get covered in bags of ice and drink tons of gatorade and water

>finally cool down after what seemed like forever

>find out I have minor permanent brain damage now because my brain was hot and swelled a lot

I wish I was joking.[113]

*The sort of thing home Bitcoin miners proudly photographed to show everyone back in the day. Source: Killhamster, Buttcoin Foundation; original source unknown.*

Further efficiency was possible. In late 2012, Butterfly Labs released mining hardware using a field-programmable gate array (FPGA), a silicon chip that you can program the circuit of. This was five times as efficient (in hashes per kilowatt-hour) as the graphics cards of the time. This was the start of industrial Bitcoin mining, and the decline of end-user mining.

Bitcoin mining was fully industrialised in 2013 with application-specific integrated circuits (ASICs). These were pretty much the FPGAs but manufactured as custom silicon chips, and were much more efficient again. The largest bitcoin miners now sponsor the development of new ASICs for their own use – since 2013, you can't compete without designing your own mining chips.

You can buy ASIC mining rigs – in May 2017, the Bitmain AntMiner S9 was $1161 for 13.5 terahash/sec at 1323 watts – but they will rapidly become obsolete, and you are unlikely to be able to turn a profit unless you have very cheap or free electricity.

(I know one person who mined at home through to 2014, keeping a close eye on electricity and hardware costs, and stopped when home mining was no longer viable even with ASICs. He came out a few hundred dollars ahead and had fun with it while there was fun to be had. This is not the usual story, however.)

From 2014 onward, the mining network was based almost entirely in China, running ASICs on very cheap subsidised local electricity. (There has long been speculation that much of this is to evade currency controls – buy electricity in yuan, sell bitcoins for dollars.[114]) On 30 June 2017, the total Bitcoin network hash rate was 5.5 exahashes per second – that's $5.5 \times 10^{18}$, or three million times the hash rate in the GPU era as of early 2011.

Everything about mining is more efficient in bulk. By the end of 2016, 75% of the Bitcoin hashrate was being generated in *one building*, using 140 megawatts[115] – or over half the estimated power used by *all* of Google's data centres worldwide at the time.[116]

There have been occasional calls to re-democratise mining by changing the hash function; some other cryptocurrencies deliberately chose hash functions that wouldn't be efficient on a graphics card or an ASIC. But it is always the case that *any* function, particularly a simple one like a hash, will be more efficient on hardware specialised to just that function than on more general-purpose hardware. And we know how to program a hash function into an FPGA for mining and then base an ASIC on it. If the Bitcoin hash were to change, new ASICs would follow with only manufacturing lead time.

## Abusing your hashpower for fun and profit

Bitcoin relies on distributed consensus: the blockchain is what a majority of mining capacity says it is. The consensus model relies on the fact that you can't outdo all the other miners casually – so it's not "secured by math," but secured by *economics*, balanced between multiple players.

Unfortunately, every force in the Bitcoin ecosystem tends to centralisation. Mining benefits from economies of scale, so it's progressed from mining on your PC, to graphics cards, to programmable chips (FPGAs), to ASICs.

Nakamoto's original Bitcoin white paper assumes a peer-to-peer network that anyone can join. In practice, the miners operate their own centralised communication pool, previously the Bitcoin Relay Network and now called the Fast Internet Bitcoin Relay Engine (FIBRE), as it's more efficient.

(This came close to being a single point of failure in January 2016, as the BRN was about to shut down from lack of funding, and the decentralised peer-to-peer network would not have been able to handle the traffic.)

As of March 2017, three pools controlled over 50% and six pools over 75% of the hash rate, with the largest individual pool at 21.3%.[117] There is no reason that multiple pools could not have a single owner. The largest mining pool owners already meet and operate as a cartel.[118]

If you control more than 50% of mining power, you can perform a "51% attack," which allows you to write the longest blockchain, which will then be taken by the rest of the network as canonical. You can double-spend confirmed transactions, or reject any new transaction you don't approve of. You can reject other miners' blocks. You can't spend someone else's bitcoins, but you can stop the owner from spending them.

Even if you have a bit less than 50%, you can still mount similar attacks with a better-than-average chance of success. From 25% of the hash rate upward, a selfish miner can mount 51%-style attacks and expect to turn a greater profit than they would otherwise.[119]

This isn't hypothetical – mining pool GHash.io went over 50% of the hash rate several times in June and July 2014.[120] GHash doing this was particularly problematic, as the pool had double-spent against a gambling site earlier that year. They blamed a rogue employee.[121]

Bitcoin decentralises things that should not be decentralised, then centralises them anyway but wastefully.

# Chapter 6: Who is Satoshi Nakamoto?

You'll know sufficient proof has been provided when it actually happens, because cryptographers will be convinced.

– Peter Todd, Bitcoin core developer[122]

The creator of Bitcoin, the pseudonymous "Satoshi Nakamoto," mined 1.1 million bitcoins over 2009 and 2010. He withdrew from the Bitcoin world and cut off contact completely in 2011. Nobody knows who he really was.

## Searching for Satoshi

Since Nakamoto's disappearance, there has been endless speculation as to his identity – as whoever was behind "Satoshi" owned 1.1 million bitcoins that haven't moved since his disappearance. The Wikipedia article on Satoshi Nakamoto even has a section listing people suspected of being him – cypherpunks Hal Finney (who had fallen ill in 2009 and died in 2014) and Nick Szabo, engineer Dorian Nakamoto, mathematician Shinichi Mochizuki …

All that is known of Nakamoto is emails and message board posts.* He even bought and edited bitcoin.org using Tor. He gave his birthdate on the P2P Foundation forums as 5 April 1975[123] and his location as Japan. He was a Windows C++ programmer. He wrote the Bitcoin white paper in OpenOffice 2.4. All of his messages are written in fluent and idiomatic English, in a single style. He was a calm, methodical and precise person, who knew his way around the use of cryptographic tools.

He may have just wanted his privacy at first, but the stalker-like tendencies of some Bitcoin fans, and obvious interest in a million-bitcoin stash, constitute excellent reasons to continue to keep his head down. The reams of Bitcoin conspiracy theorist projection and pareidolia that followed single derived "facts" like a birth date is

---

\* The Satoshi Nakamoto Institute site collects every public post by him, and emails people have released.

frankly disturbing,[124] and even better reason not to want to leave oneself exposed.

(Gwern Branwen, a writer who ferreted out Nakamoto's apparent birth date, discovered this when an incoherent but persistent Bitcoiner tried to threaten and blackmail *him* in late 2013 on the assumption that he was Satoshi.[125] "Gwern Branwen" is also a pseudonym, by the way.)

Bitcoin advocates worry that such a large pool of bitcoins coming into play would massively destabilise the Bitcoin world, and – per Bitcoin economic theories – cause massive devaluation of bitcoins due to the sudden supply increase. (Though what would probably happen is that everyone would just pretend everything was fine, and keep speculating, buying drugs and paying to unlock their PCs from ransomware – there are already plenty of Bitcoin "whales" with enough coins to destabilise the price if they wanted to.) Since every Bitcoin transaction is visible on the blockchain, there are those who watch the blockchain like hawks for those bitcoins ever moving.

If someone comes forward claiming to be Satoshi Nakamoto, there is precisely one thing people are interested in: do they control those bitcoins? If they can move even a fraction of a bitcoin from Nakamoto's pile to someone else, they are Satoshi Nakamoto. Or they could sign a message using the PGP private key (a cryptographic key for signing email messages) that matched the PGP public key that Nakamoto had put on the front of bitcoin.org in 2008. If they can't, they aren't Satoshi.

## Dorian Nakamoto

News magazine *Newsweek* had been sold off as a debt-ridden liability in 2010 and stopped print publication in 2012. It was sold again in late 2013 and relaunched in print in March 2014. It led the relaunch with what seemed a major scoop: after two months of investigation, Newsweek journalists had identified a 64-year-old engineer from Los Angeles, Dorian Prentice Satoshi Nakamoto, as the Satoshi Nakamoto who had created Bitcoin.[126]

Dorian Nakamoto was not impressed. As reporters gathered outside his house, he offered an interview to the first one who would buy him lunch – "Wait a minute, I want my free lunch first. I'm going with this guy" – and, after a reporter car chase through LA, spoke to the Associated Press denying any involvement in or knowledge of Bitcoin.[127] The quote that Newsweek claimed as an admission of being Satoshi was "I am no longer involved in that and I cannot discuss it. It's been turned over to other people. They are in charge of it now. I no longer have any connection." However, he said that he had been speaking of his work on classified systems for military contractors, and that he hadn't even heard of Bitcoin (which he first called "Bitcom" with an M) until his son had been contacted by a reporter two months earlier.

In the first sighting since 2011, the "Satoshi Nakamoto" account that had posted the 2009 announcement of Bitcoin 0.1 on the P2P Foundation forums commented on that post: "I am not Dorian Nakamoto." (Some noted that the comment could have been posted by a forum administrator and that it was not cryptographically confirmed to be Satoshi Nakamoto.)[128] The Bitcoin world was both utterly unconvinced by *Newsweek*'s report, and outraged that they would violate an alleged Satoshi Nakamoto's privacy in that manner.[129] [130]

*Newsweek* defended its article,[131] but eventually appended a statement from Dorian Nakamoto to the web version of the original piece in which he denied the whole story and noted the damage it had done to his livelihood.

## Professor Dr Dr Craig Wright: Nakamoto Dundee. That's not a signature.

Craig Wright is an Australian computer businessman. He claimed in 2016 to be Satoshi Nakamoto. He didn't move a bitcoin from the Satoshi stash or successfully sign a message using a known Satoshi Nakamoto key – instead, he did absolutely everything else except those things, in ways that didn't check out and which others immediately spotted the problems in.*

Wright's LinkedIn page (since deleted) at the end of 2015 listed multiple master's degrees, a doctorate in theology from an unnamed university and a doctorate in computer science from Charles Sturt University earned during his five years as an unpaid adjunct lecturer

---

\* Further reading for this section: Nik Cubrilovic. "Craig Wright is not Satoshi Nakamoto". 2 May 2016. A comprehensive overview of the evidence concerning Wright's claims.

(along with three more master's in that time). This second doctorate turns out not to have yet been awarded, CSU saying that the doctoral thesis was still being considered.[132] (It was finally accepted in February 2017.[133]) The text of the profile was peppered with typographical and grammatical errors. At the top of the work history, it stated: "July 2015 – Present (6 months): Writing papers, Research, Managing change. Nothing but security and blockchain."

Wright had been active on the Cypherpunks mailing list in 1996,[134] so he may have been aware of the ongoing currency discussions. In February 2011, he blogged that central banks had "devalued all our savings and capital investments" through "printing money", leading to a resurgence of interest in the gold standard.[135] He then proposed a PayPal-like system backed with gold. In the comments he emphasised "The sole basis is in a currency that cannot be printed like paper." Imagine someone writing this if they had *invented Bitcoin* two years before.

The first time Wright is known to have spoken of Bitcoin was in the comments of his August 2011 post on *The Conversation*, "LulzSec, Anonymous … freedom fighters or the new face of evil?" in which he wrote of "Bit Coin" as a solution to WikiLeaks' problems receiving donations.[136]

Wright started buying bitcoins on Mt. Gox in April 2013, including 17.24 BTC at the peak of the bubble in November for $1198 each.[137] Some time in 2013, he posted backdated entries to his personal blog with references to Bitcoin and Bitcoin-related concepts:

- A post dated August 2008 mentions he will be releasing a "cryptocurrency paper" and references "Triple Entry Accounting,"[138] a 2005 paper by financial cryptographer Ian Grigg.

- One post dated November 2008 includes a PGP key owned by *satoshin@vistomail.com* – one letter different from *satoshi@vistomail.com,* an address the real Nakamoto had been known to use. This PGP key used a cipher suite not used in PGP at the time, and wasn't on the public key servers in 2011, which suggests the key had also been backdated.[139]

- Finally, dated 10 January 2009 (it would have been 9 January in the US), there was this post:

**Bitcoin**

Well, e-gold is down the toilet. Good idea, but again centralised authority.

The Beta of Bitcoin is live tomorrow. This is decentralized … We try until it works.

Some good coders on this. The paper rocks. http://www.bitcoin.org/bitcoin.pdf

Wright established the company Hotwire PE in 2013 with the stated purpose of research and development work using e-learning and e-payment software. Hotwire bought the software from Wright's own Wright Family Trust. Hotwire was capitalised by Wright with AUD$30 million in bitcoins. (It's not clear if these existed; this would have been 1.5% of all bitcoins at the time.) AUD$29 million of this was paid (still in bitcoins) to Wright's trust to buy software. This incurred sales tax (GST). Hotwire then claimed a GST refund of AUD$3.1 million on this R&D expense – which would have been received from the Australian Tax Office in actual dollars.

The ATO was unimpressed with these arrangements and withheld the refund pending investigation,[140] eventually assessing a AUD$1.7 million penalty. The mid-2014 administrator's report for Hotwire PE noted the company was capitalised only with bitcoins, with its only assets being anticipated tax rebates, and blamed the company's failure on the collapse of Mt. Gox.

Wright had also applied for an R&D incentive scheme, where a company could receive its tax rebate in advance. His company DeMorgan claimed in 2015 that it was eligible for up to AUD$54 million for a supercomputer "dedicated to Cryptocurrency and smart contract research".[141]

In June 2015, Wright got his former colleague Stefan Matthews to put him in touch with Robert MacGregor of Canadian money transmitter nTrust. Matthews told MacGregor that Wright was almost certainly Satoshi Nakamoto. MacGregor was working with Canadian gambling billionaire Calvin Ayre, who Matthews had also previously worked for.

On 29 June 2015, MacGregor and Ayre signed a deal to buy Wright's companies and his claimed blockchain patents and clear his debts, legal fees and employees' back wages, and form a research unit led by Wright that they could sell to a larger company. They also set out to market "Satoshi Nakamoto"'s life story, and commissioned novelist and journalist Andrew O'Hagan to write a biography. O'Hagan didn't take their money and refused to sign a nondisclosure agreement, but instead pursued the story as an embedded but independent journalist. He eventually published a book-length article on Wright in the *London Review of Books*.[142]

(Matthews told O'Hagan that Wright had shown him the 2008 Bitcoin white paper before publication, though Wright's February 2011 blog post makes it seem startlingly unlikely that Wright had heard of Bitcoin that early. Wright had also told Matthews he had met with Ross Ulbricht of the Silk Road in Sydney. O'Hagan notes: "MacGregor later told me he was convinced because Wright had shown Matthews the draft Satoshi white paper. 'I always had that,' MacGregor said.")

In November 2015, an anonymous source began sending documents about Wright and Bitcoin to Gwern Branwen. Branwen provided the documents to Andy Greenberg at *Wired*.[143] A similar document stash was sent to journalists at *Gizmodo*. "I hacked Satoshi Nakamoto [*sic*]. These files are all from his business account. The person is Dr Craig Wright."[144] Document drops had been sent to others, including the *New York Times* and Nathaniel Popper, author of Bitcoin history *Digital Gold;* none considered the story sufficiently credible to pursue. Leah McGrath Goodman at *Newsweek* noted that "it was being shopped around fairly aggressively this autumn."[145]

*Gizmodo* speculated that Wright and Dave Kleiman – a computer security and forensics expert and author who had died in April 2013 – had together been "Satoshi". Wright had co-authored some of Kleiman's security study guides and claimed he had been a close friend.

As well as pointers to the earlier backdated blog entries, the "leaked" documents included:

- a scanned PDF of an unsigned document with Kleiman's name on it, dated 6 September 2011, purporting to set up a trust, the Tulip Trust, backed by 1,100,111 BTC, controlled by Kleiman and locked until 2020. (The Satoshi stash being locked in a trust answered MacGregor's question "why isn't he sitting on an island surrounded by piles of gold?") The document includes the note "The amount not included will be used to show the 'lies and fraud perpetuated by Adam Westwood of the Australian Tax Office against Dr Wright'".[146]

- an unverified transcript of interviews between Wright and his lawyer and the Australian Tax Office, including claims that Wright had been mining bitcoins since 2009, and how he had

"1.1 million Bitcoins. There was a point in time, when he had around 10% of all the Bitcoins out there. Mr Kleiman would have had a similar amount."[147]

- emails purportedly from 2009 discussing cryptocurrency-related ideas with Kleiman.

- a letter from supercomputer vendor SGI to Wright's company Cloudcroft saying it would be assisting in the development of "hyper-density machines" (whatever those are; the term appears only to be used by or around Wright).[148]

The documents and claims were greeted with widespread skepticism, particularly given the backdated blog posts and the technical details that failed to check out. News site *Fusion* went so far as to assert outright that Wright had likely sent the "leak" himself.[149] SGI said it had never had any contact with Cloudcroft or Wright.[150] Cloudcroft's C01N had been No. 17 on the November 2015 *Top500* list of the world's most powerful computers, although it has since been removed from that month's list;[151] *Top500* declined to detail how they'd verified this entry.

A few hours after the *Wired* and *Gizmodo* stories became worldwide news, Wright's house and office were raided by police on behalf of the ATO, though they stated the raid was "unrelated to recent mass media reporting".[152] Wright and his wife had moved out the day before; Wright told O'Hagan of skipping the country just in time to evade the police. The ATO continued investigating through the next few months; they firmly believed "Wright is not the creator of Bitcoin and that he may have created the hoax to distract from his tax issues."[153]

Wright deleted his online social media presence and did not respond to media queries. Nothing more was heard from him for a few months; he was in the London office of nCrypt, the subsidiary nTrust had created for him, working on blockchain-related patents.

He spoke at length to O'Hagan at this time about his life and work; O'Hagan noted that Wright "had a habit of dissembling, of now and then lying about small things in a way that cast shade on larger things":

> Wright told me that around this time he was in correspondence with Wei Dai, with Gavin Andresen, who would go on to lead the development of bitcoin, and Mike Hearn, a Google engineer who had ideas about the direction bitcoin should take. Yet when I asked for copies of the emails

between Satoshi and these men he said they had been wiped when he was running from the ATO. It seemed odd, and still does, that some emails were lost while others were not.

Allen Pedersen, who worked for Wright both in Australia and at nCrypt, told O'Hagan:

> He's sold his soul ... They can't just sign all these papers and think it's going to be all right, that they'll sort something out. It doesn't work that way. They now have to go to the end and live with it. But they're doing it on first class. When this Satoshi thing comes out I can see a lot of bad things happening, and they are not geared up for this, any of them ... There's not really a happy ending here ... in Australia you could say he was in control. He's learned absolutely nothing. He's now in this box, he can't move, he can't do anything, and this box is getting smaller and smaller.

Gavin Andresen had taken over as lead Bitcoin developer when Nakamoto abandoned the project. He had communicated at length with Nakamoto in the early days. Wright convinced him he might be Nakamoto by writing emails in his usual style, and then the same content in Nakamoto's style.

Andresen went to London to meet with Wright. Wright cryptographically signed a message as Satoshi Nakamoto on his own computer and verified it. Andresen wanted to check it on *his* computer, saying he had to be able to say that he'd checked it independently. Wright suddenly balked, not trusting Andresen's hardware. A new laptop was obtained and unwrapped and Wright installed the Bitcoin Electrum wallet software.* Wright opened the claimed Satoshi Nakamoto Bitcoin wallet on the new laptop and seemed to verify that he held a Satoshi Nakamoto private key.[154] Wright performed a similar demonstration for Jon Matonis from the Bitcoin Foundation.[155] None of this evidence was released for public review; Andresen said "I was not allowed to keep the message or laptop (fear it would leak before Official Announcement)."[156]

The PR team secured the BBC, *The Economist* and *GQ*; the journalists signed non-disclosure agreements and embargoes, and in late April Wright demonstrated use of the Satoshi key to each. O'Hagan noted how oddly convoluted all this was, given that

---

\* This has been hypothesised as a way to fake the signing, *e.g.*, a Reddit discussion thread started by Electrum developer EagleTM: comment on "Gavin explains how Craig Wright convinced him". Reddit /r/bitcoin, 2 May 2016.

everyone knew that all Wright had to do was send an email signed with a Satoshi PGP key or move a bitcoin from the Satoshi stash and the entire Internet would light up. "I felt distinctly that there was something missing and something wrong."

On Monday 2 May 2016 at 8:00am, Wright posted to his blog a Jean-Paul Sartre speech claimed to be signed with a Satoshi PGP key, and Andresen posted that he believed Wright was Satoshi. Rory Cellan-Jones from the BBC, Calvin Ayre and *The Economist* tweeted. A segment from Cellan-Jones aired on the BBC Radio 4 *Today* programme, the most important current affairs radio show in the UK. The story blanketed the media.

By midday, the Internet had analysed the evidence and was not impressed. Wright's blog post was not signed with a Satoshi key – it was clearly faked: an old signature from the blockchain had been copied and pasted onto the message.[157] Wright's name became a punchline.

Nobody could work out what was up with Wright – he had considerable supporting evidence of being Satoshi Nakamoto, except the cryptographic evidence that would nail the proof; and the real Satoshi would know very well that that was the only thing that would nail the proof.

The money men were not pleased, but worked on how to recover the situation. "This is what we're going to do, because he knew the next move was pack your toothbrush and get on a plane and good luck in Australia," MacGregor told O'Hagan.

On Tuesday 3 May, Wright posted to his blog that he would move a bitcoin from the Satoshi stash. On Wednesday 4 May, the nCrypt team organised for Wright to send bitcoins from the Satoshi stash to Andresen and Cellan-Jones at the BBC. Wright said to Andresen that he was worried about a security flaw in the early blockchain that would expose him to theft if he moved an early bitcoin; Andresen said the problem had been fixed, but Wright continued to worry.

On Thursday, Wright sent around an email link to a news story from *SiliconAngle:* "Craig Wright faces criminal charges and serious jail time in UK" – that he would be arrested as the creator of Bitcoin for enabling terrorism. "I am the source of terrorist funds as bitcoin creator or I am a fraud to the world. At least a fraud is able to see his family. There is nothing I can do." He closed his blog and posted a final goodbye message, apologising for disappointing everyone.

The news story turned out to be a fake, posted on an impostor site but with the design from the *SiliconAngle* site.[*] The fake quickly disappeared; nobody knows the source.

Many noted that Wright's story would all make sense if Dave Kleiman had been the main technical "Satoshi Nakamoto," and Wright had started by stretching his own involvement in the creation of Bitcoin and got in over his head. But, though Kleiman, as a security expert, was familiar with cryptography, there was no evidence during his life that he had any interest in cryptocurrency or C++ programming, let alone Bitcoin – every word of such came via Wright, sources close to Wright or the *Wired*/*Gizmodo* "leaker."

Wright disappeared from the public eye, though he did file various blockchain-related patents.[158] [159] He emerged again in early 2017 with nChain[160] (the new name for nCrypt, originally EITC), with Robert MacGregor, Allen Pedersen[161] and Jon Matonis[162] in tow.

In late June 2017 he spoke at the Future of Bitcoin Conference (where he was introduced as "Bitcoin Dundee") and threatened legal action against those who had called him a "fraud;"[†] this led to a burst of people, including Bitcoin core developer Peter Todd,[163] calling him a fraud. He refused to be drawn on his previous claims to be Satoshi.

---

[*] "Craig Wright faces criminal charges and serious jail time in UK after claiming to be Bitcoin's founder Satoshi Nakamoto". The fake site's URL was silliconangle.com, with two Ls.

[†] "Craig Wright at the 2017 Future of Bitcoin Conference". YouTube. Quote at 1:14:38: "I'm a pariah. I am an evil person that some people like to call fraud. Some of those are going to discover the legal consequences very cert– ah, sure … well, I won't say exactly when, and I won't say who quite yet, but they're coming."

# Chapter 7: Spending bitcoins in 2017

The only use case for which Bitcoin even rivals conventional financial systems is illicit goods and services – mostly drugs – and computer ransoms. Illegal drugs on the darknet have been the primary non-speculation use case since the Silk Road started in January 2011, reaching an estimated $14.2 million in the month of January 2016[164] (or $170 million a year). They were overtaken by ransomware some time in 2016 – the FBI estimates ransomware payments at $1 billion in 2016.[165] All use cases, licit and illicit, are severely hampered by the perennial transaction backlog.

## Bitcoin is full: the transaction clog

The Bitcoin block size is 1 megabyte per 10 minutes, which allows a theoretical maximum of 7 transactions per second. Transactions were cheap and fast for many years – but by mid-2015, the blocks were often full. Suddenly there were delays and increasing fees. Bitcoin had reached capacity for the few users it had.

This rapidly became the new normal. The FAQ on bitcoin.org changed from "Very low fees … no fees or extremely small fees" up to 29 July 2015 to "Low fees" on 4 August 2015 and "Choose your own fees" on 7 August 2015.[166]

What this means is that users are in a blind auction, where they have to guess bigger and bigger fees in the hope of getting their transaction through. Transactions are routinely delayed hours or days, so many just get lost. (Only 57% of transactions are confirmed in the first hour; 20% never get confirmed at all, and are eventually dropped.[167])

It didn't help when some people on Reddit /r/bitcoin thought they'd stress-test the blockchain in May 2015. They sent out a flood of complex chained transactions, which sent confirmation times from ten minutes up to *eight hours* at a cost of 2.4 BTC in fees (only a few hundred dollars at the time).[168] Interestingly, this attack didn't even fill many of the blocks – just the "mempool" ("memory pool" – the backlog of transactions to be processed).[169]

A July attack sent hundreds of transactions per second with a low value but a large message field, taking up space in the blocks.[170] In October, an attacker sent a flood of 88,000 transactions, filling the mempool on some network nodes and knocking 16% of nodes offline.[171] Attacks continued through 2016.[172]

These days spam attacks are largely superfluous, as clogged transactions are just part of Bitcoin. By October 2016, Bitcoin regularly had around 40,000 unconfirmed transactions in the mempool at any time, and in May 2017 it peaked at 200,000.[173]

The possible solutions are:

1. Increase the block size, which will increase centralisation even further – big blocks take longer to propagate, and the blockchain becomes even more unwieldy. (Though that ship really sailed in 2013).

2. *Sidechains:* bolt on a completely different non-Bitcoin cryptocurrency, and do all the real transactions there. (This is presently vapourware.) It is unclear why anyone would create a usable alternate cryptocurrency then peg it to Bitcoin, rather than just use it in its own right.

3. *The Lightning Network:* bolt on a completely different non-Bitcoin network, and do all the real transactions there. (This is also vapourware.)

4. Use a different cryptocurrency that hasn't clogged yet. (The darknets are exploring this option.)

The Bitcoin community is now sufficiently dysfunctional that even such a simple proposal as "OK, let's increase the block size to *two* megabytes" led to community schisms, code forks, retributive DDOS attacks, death threats,[174] a split between the Chinese miners and the American core programmers ... and plenty of other clear evidence that this and other problems in the Bitcoin protocol will *never* be fixed by a consensus process.

On the other hand, just increasing the block size won't fix Bitcoin's architecture, and the blocks will rapidly fill again – going by the trend from 2013 to 2015, blocks would be averaging around 1.6 megabytes by mid-2017 – and the blockchain will grow even faster.

Bitcoin was the cardboard-and-string proof of concept for the idea of cryptocurrency, that was then pressed into production use. It's amazing it held up in real use as long as it did.

## Bitcoin for drugs: welcome to the darknet

The darknet markets are fuelled by users who want to buy drugs without having to go to the bad part of town and talk to people from a minority, and dealers obtaining commercial quantities to sell locally. Although it's less than 0.1% of the global drug economy,[*] Bitcoin is visibly a part of contemporary drug culture. Drug paraphernalia stores even have "Buy Bitcoin here" signs.

*Skunk House, Croydon, UK. Photo: ©2016 Karen Boyd.*
*"TBF to them, they have now taken down the Bitcoin decals as even they have decided it's bobbins." – Karen Boyd, 2017.*

---

[*] Rand Corporation's estimate of the darknet drug market as $14.2m in January 2016 ("Internet-facilitated drugs trade: An analysis of the size, scope and the role of the Netherlands". Rand Corporation, 2016) would make it $170m/year; the UN Office on Drugs and Crime estimated the whole global illegal drug market at $321.6 billion in 2003, and presumably more now. All these figures are extremely rubbery (which may be why the latest global figure is from 2003), but "less than 0.1%" seems a safe statement. "World Drug Report 2005: Volume 1: Analysis". United Nations Office on Drugs and Crime. p. 127. ISBN 92-1-148200-3.

Darknet markets remain the most popular Bitcoin use case after speculation and ransomware. In 2014, darknet markets were estimated to have processed more bitcoins than all legitimate payment processors put together.[175]

Gwern Branwen has written extensively on the darknet markets and has released 1.6 terabytes of screenshots from darknet sites,[176] with analyses.[177] The darknet markets fulfil a demand (drugs), but, despite increasingly complex escrow arrangements, they still fall to bad operational security or getting hacked, or just steal all their users' money – "the constant wearying turmoil of exit-scams and hacks".[178] That said, reliability and quality remain surprisingly good otherwise.

However, even drug buyers avoid Bitcoin if they possibly can. Both buyers and sellers frequently complain of Bitcoin's ridiculously volatile price messing up deals, and transactions taking hours or days to be confirmed with an unpredictable fee. Some small darknet markets allow minor cryptocurrencies like Monero. In May 2017, AlphaBay, the largest darknet market, started offering Ethereum as an option[179] – because Bitcoin was failing to serve its primary consumer use case.

## Ransomware

Ransomware combines computer malware, encryption and anonymous payment systems. Malicious software spreads through email spam or exploiting computer security holes; it encrypts the files on your Windows PC and any shared folders it can access, and a message pops up telling you to send Bitcoins to the hacker's address (usually an address per victim) to get the key to unlock your system before the deadline of a few days.

Bitcoin is now the payment channel of choice, but ransomware existed for decades before Bitcoin. The first extortion malware was the "AIDS Trojan" or "PC Cyborg Trojan" in 1989, which would hide in the AUTOEXEC.BAT file on a DOS PC and, the ninetieth time it was run, encrypt all filenames on the disk and demand you send $189 to a post office box in Panama. Later payment schemes included e-Gold or Liberty Reserve, premium rate SMS messages or international phone calls, or buying particular medicines on a particular website.[180] The 2011 "police virus" pretended to be from the local police force and demanded payment by credit card.[181] The

2013 "FBI MoneyPak" ransomware demanded payment via online money transfer services MoneyPak or Ukash.

CryptoLocker, the first ransomware to use Bitcoin (though you could also pay by Moneypak or Ukash), showed up in September 2013. It was hugely successful, taking about $3 million, and spawned many imitators.

Security professionals I spoke to say that the reason for the explosion in ransomware from about 2015 on is not Bitcoin (as media reports often claim), but the ready availability of ransomware builders in malware kits from the hacker underground since that time – so that any script-kiddie can use a kit to make their own ransomware.

The best-known ransomware of late is probably WannaCry. The WannaCry attack of 12 May 2017 knocked out several NHS hospitals in the UK and companies around the world. It used a Microsoft Windows vulnerability that had been fixed in March, but many organisations had not updated their Windows installations.

Some victims have tremendous difficulty obtaining the bitcoins to pay the ransom – most exchanges have strong identity verification requirements, and often the delay before allowing trades is longer than the ransomware's deadline. Not to mention the frequent delays getting Bitcoin transactions through at all.

Bitcoins are so hard for normal people to use that from CryptoLocker on, ransomware operators have been known to provide technical support to victims, so they can work out how to pay them and unlock their files. F-Secure even compiled a customer service evaluation of ransomware gangs.[182]

Citrix ran a promotional survey in 2016[183] and again in 2017[184] suggesting that some UK companies were keeping Bitcoins on hand just in case it happened to them – though paying ransoms is not recommended,[185] as victims often don't get their files back even then, and paying up marks you as a future target; Telstra's "2017 Cyber Security Report" said that a third of surveyed Australian organisations who paid the ransom didn't get their files back.[186] Victims are, unsurprisingly, increasingly reluctant to trust the good will of organised criminal gangs; WannaCry infected PCs around the world and only took in $80,000.

IT professionals recommend keeping Windows fully updated for security, and keeping reliable daily backups, so that if you're hit you can just wipe the PC and restore your data. When the NHS was hit by WannaCry, no patient data was stored on the affected machines and they did not pay the ransom – they just spent the next day reimaging thousands of PCs afresh.[187]

Bitcoin seems to be the only cryptocurrency used by ransomware so far – though one WannaCry imitator mined the altcoin Monero on infected PCs.[188]

If you do get an apparent infection, it's worth checking it isn't *fake* ransomware, that locks your screen and demands your money, but doesn't bother with encrypting your files.[189]

The WannaCry attack was sufficiently egregious that some started calling for Bitcoin to be banned altogether, since its non-speculation uses are largely illegal. One exchange, Coin.mx, had even been charged in 2015 with money laundering violations for selling bitcoins to the *victims* of ransomware attacks, as this enabled the criminals to get paid for them – though this was as part of a long list of other money-laundering charges.[190]

## Non-illegal goods and services

For ordinary people to regard Bitcoin as money, shops other than darknet drug markets have to accept it. Advocates are very keen on merchant adoption, because it spreads Bitcoin's name in the wider world and makes it look useful. Unfortunately, approximately none of them buy things with bitcoins themselves.

The way the process usually works is:

- advocates lobby a merchant to accept Bitcoin;
- the merchant says no;
- advocates harass the merchant.

If they do accept:

- the merchant sets up a mechanism to accept Bitcoin – usually via BitPay, Coinbase or a similar payment processor who will give them dollars, meaning they never touch a bitcoin themselves;
- after an initial burst, nobody much uses it;
- advocates protest loudly at the merchant dropping Bitcoin.

The advocates tend to hold their coins rather than spending them, in order to cash in when *other* people have increased demand and raised the price. Prominent Bitcoin advocates have even worried that *too much* merchant adoption might drop the value of their holding.[191]

The general public don't buy bitcoins to spend on anything they could just buy in ordinary money, and without waiting hours or days for the transaction to confirm. All but a very few merchant adoptions fall by the wayside.

*Cards Against Humanity* in 2013 was a typical example of Bitcoin outreach in practice. *Cards Against Humanity* is a card game that you can buy mail-order, or just download the PDFs to print out yourself. One Bitcoiner asked if he could buy a pack with bitcoins; when they said no, he emailed back pressing the point and stressing the "exposure" value this would offer them. (Of course, every creator knows that when you offer them "exposure," that means you have no intention of paying them.)

When they replied demurring once more, the Bitcoiner complained to his fellow advocates on Reddit /r/bitcoin.[192] "I wasn't expecting them to do a single sale in Bitcoins just for me but instead I wanted them to consider doing business using bitcoins and potentially benefit from the publicity that might come with that."

One commenter posted: "They just prefer the imaginary debt based 'money' their slavemasters issue via the central banks of the world." (Max Temkin of *Cards Against Humanity* responded: "Yes I use it to buy groceries."[193]) Another suggested continuing to email them: "Hey OP, if you really want to prove your point to the sellers of this game, you should: Once a month send an email detailing how much the Bitcoin you would have sent in payment for the game has increased in value, compared to how much the USD has decreased in value due to inflation. After awhile they just might understand." Others harassed Temkin on his blog and threatened further action on Reddit.[194]

When merchants do adopt Bitcoin, it tends not to result in a flood of business. Australian phone app MyBus, for local bus travel in Canberra, added Bitcoin as an option in March 2014, and had twenty-three transactions total by the time they removed it in January 2015. When they temporarily switched off the option for maintenance in September 2014, they received "about 30 emails from people asking for it to be reinstalled, which is odd because that's more people than have actually used the feature."[195]

Automattic, the company that develops blogging software WordPress, offered Bitcoin in November 2012 to allow paid wordpress.com upgrades for users without access to PayPal or credit cards. They withdrew the option in February 2015, noting it was only used approximately twice a week.[196]

The Mozilla Foundation, the charity that develops the Firefox web browser, began accepting Bitcoin donations for their end of 2014 campaign. This wasn't good enough for the advocates: they demanded Mozilla include Bitcoin prominently on the primary donation page! With millions of page views, it was quite easy to run an A/B test, where you serve a different version of the page to a fraction of the viewers and can directly compare the effects of the two versions. The A/B test showed that the text "Donate with Bitcoin" *dropped* revenue per visitor by 7.5%; adding the text would have lost them $140,000 over the campaign, for the sake of a few thousand dollars in Bitcoin.[197] The Bitcoin community, of course, claimed that this literal direct measurement was somehow statistically bogus, listing objections that showed they didn't understand what an A/B test was.[198]

The Wikimedia Foundation (the charity behind Wikipedia) did rather better, accepting Bitcoin via Coinbase from August 2014; by August 2015 they had taken $220,000, though $140,000 of that was in the first week.[199] Wikimedia didn't A/B test Bitcoin on the primary page, only listing it at the end of the secondary "Ways to Give" page.

(This was after some problematic interactions with Bitcoin advocates. One member of the Wikimedia fundraising team noted in January 2014: "The bitcoin community should be aware that their persistent and often times aggressive, rude, and vulgar messaging towards me and my fellow coworkers is not appreciated; nor does it help their cause."[200])

Overstock.com started accepting Bitcoin in early 2014 because CEO Patrick Byrne is a huge Bitcoin fan, and took in $1 million in the first month[201] and another $2 million over the rest of 2014 − 0.2% of its total sales of $1.5 billion[202] − though a loss of $117,000 on cryptocurrencies for 2015.[203]

WhollyHemp, a small manufacturer of hemp soap, started accepting Bitcoin out of interest in the technology, and founder Robert Lestak was for a time a moderator of Reddit /r/bitcoin. After the usual initial burst,[204] WhollyHemp ended up making 0.2% of sales in Bitcoin, and an A/B test showed that prominent mention of Bitcoin acceptance *reduced* gross sales by 5.8%.[205] They removed the Bitcoin option altogether in April 2015, and were harassed by Bitcoin advocates[206] for the next several months.[207] Lestak: "This is why you don't hear about businesses publicly dropping Bitcoin as a payment option. Bitcoiners will make your life a living hell if you do."

*"Mr. Bitcoin" at the Bitcoin Bowl. Photo: ©2014 Ben Gutzler.*

Hoping to drum up business with merchants, payment processor BitPay sponsored the St. Petersburg Bowl, a minor college football game, naming the 2014 game the Bitcoin Bowl. You couldn't use Bitcoin in the stadium at all; a few attendees were interested, but almost nobody knew or cared what this thing was, or thought "Bitcoin" was a company[208] – St. Petersburg presented a key to the city to "the chair of Bitcoin".[209] BitPay claimed almost a hundred local businesses had signed up – but very few saw significant sales, and nearly half saw zero.[210] A year later, local Bitcoin retail trade was almost nonexistent.[211]

The game was played on a baseball field with terrible turf, and the football fans were unimpressed. The main interest was the mascot, Mr. Bitcoin, a man dressed up as a physical bitcoin, running around the bleachers attempting to whip up excitement.

Though originally a three-year deal, the sponsorship was ended after just one year, BitPay having had to lay off several employees shortly after the event.

## Case study: Individual Pubs

Individual Pubs, a small UK pub chain, is the most successful Bitcoin merchant adoption I know of. Steve Early is a Cambridge computer scientist and beer enthusiast turned publican. He writes all his own till software and control systems for the pubs. (The only pub chain ever to get a six-page writeup in a Linux magazine.[212]) When he said in mid-2013 that he was thinking about Bitcoin, I considered he was the one person I knew who was most likely to do well out of it. The pub corporation sells the coins to Steve at the BitPay rate for that day, Steve sells them at his leisure.

It was actually easier to process bitcoins than cards: "I was so frustrated, and still am, with the inability to integrate card payments with the tills. This seems to be a uniquely UK thing – the banks own the terminals. You always have to rent them from the bank or a reseller. They configure the terminal, you don't get an API to it. This is why Britain was able to go chip-and-PIN so quickly – the banks could just replace the terminals without having to convince the merchants.

"In June 2013, I was relief-managing our pub in Norwich and I was bored. Adding Bitcoin to the tills was two evenings of hacking. There were a couple of weeks of testing and refinement, and it's basically been untouched since then, except when an interface changes.[213] I did it to scratch the itch, not for publicity or profit.

"Takings stayed high for about nine months, about £1000 a month out of a couple of hundred thousand across the chain. Currently it's about £200 a month, which I suspect represents two or three customers. Since I've started, I've taken about £17,000 worth.

"I am accepting Bitcoin in the most naive manner possible, accepting zero-confirmation transactions." *(Where you can see someone's tried a transaction, but it hasn't made it into a block yet; vulnerable to fraudulent customers double-spending.)* "Which is pretty much the only way it can work in a pub setting. Zero confirmation has worked out so far. There's been *one* occasion where a transaction wasn't confirmed.

"The transaction backlog getting bigger and bigger as the block size stays the same is going to be a problem. A hundred percent of your customers can be honest, and you can still lose out because your transactions are dropped. When too many are dropped, that's when I'll have to push the off switch. I have probably more than recovered that from people accidentally paying twice because we didn't think the transaction went through the first time. For comparison, we take about fifty quid of bogus notes a year. I've turned off Bitcoin transactions at all the pubs except the Pembury and Queen Edith; the other pubs were getting more failed transactions than successful ones."

# Chapter 8: Trading bitcoins in 2017: the second crypto bubble

If you want to trade bitcoins, or crypto assets in general, in 2017, approach it like penny stocks, only with less regulation or substance. These are extremely risky assets. If you don't seriously know your stuff, you will be the one other people make their money from.

Approximately 95% of on-chain transactions are day traders on Chinese exchanges;[214] Western Bitcoin advocates are functionally a sideshow, apart from the actual coders who work on the Bitcoin core software.

## How to get bitcoins

If you don't mine bitcoins yourself or sell a product or service for bitcoins, you'll need to buy them. This can be fraught. Even the mostly-unregulated exchanges want to be able to convert to US dollars, so they comply with US Know Your Customer anti-money-laundering laws (KYC/AML), demand trustworthy government identification – and remember that you're often sending this to people you know nothing about – and will cut off your account if they think you're doing anything even slightly suspect. (Coinbase ask to verify your US bank account by *logging into it as you*.[215])

You can buy bitcoins without ID at a price premium (and much greater risk) from less trustworthy sources, such as a business deal in a parking lot with someone you met on LocalBitcoins – those always work out well.

You can buy bitcoins *with* ID at a price premium (and some risk) from a Bitcoin ATM, if you find one that works properly, and you're prepared to wait ages for anything to happen. These used to be far easier to use, but then the authorities realised they were handy street-corner money-laundering devices and started requiring KYC/AML-quality identification.

Other cryptocurrencies can be bought similarly, or you can buy bitcoins and then buy the other coin with those.

Some banks in the UK[216] and Australia[217] have closed accounts for Bitcoin-related activity – it has a stigma as a currency widely used for questionable transactions.

## From the first bubble to the second

After the 2013 bubble and 2014 price crash, people lost interest and the trading volume declined. The price slowly rose again and was $630 by mid-October 2016 and bubbled to a peak of $3000 in June 2017 – but large holders trying to sell their bitcoins risk causing a flash crash; the "price" is not realisable for any substantial quantity. The market remains thin enough that single traders can send the price up or down $30,[218] and an April 2017 crash from $1180 to 6 cents (due to configuration errors on Coinbase's GDAX exchange) was courtesy 100 BTC of trades.[219]

As well as drugs and ransomware, non-speculative usage includes various "Republic of Bitcoin" schemes run by the infamous Russian MMM concern, who perpetrated the largest Ponzi in history in the 1990s. After starting up again in 2011, they adopted Bitcoin in 2015, running schemes in China and Nigeria.

The price rise during 2016 without organic volume was helped along by "painting the tape," in which automated systems trade in a coordinated manner to push the price up. The "Willybot" and "Markus" bots were notorious on Mt. Gox from the end of 2013 until its closure, and appeared to be operating even when the exchange was offline.[220] There were accusations of similar tape-painting in 2016 between Chinese exchanges OKCoin and Huobi.[221] As soon as Chinese regulators stopped by in early 2017 to look at what the local exchanges were actually doing, both price[222] and on-exchange transaction volume[223] collapsed and withdrawals were suspended for a month.[224] MMM's Nigerian scheme also pushed the price up in late 2016.[225]

The quoted price of Bitcoin – typically a weighted average of exchange spot prices[226] – has been observed going up even when the blockchain was getting hammered with transaction spam, when non-spam transactions were all but impossible; this was activity entirely inside the individual exchanges, without reference to the outside world.

If you're online when you're reading this section, go to Cryptowat.ch,[227] a list of prices at various exchanges, and look at the spreads. Bitcoin is not short on programmers who can automate obvious arbitrage opportunities, so spreads like that directly indicate just how hard it is in practice to get your actual money (and sometimes your bitcoins) out of the exchanges.

The price rose dizzyingly in a second major bubble in mid-2017, going from $900 in April to around $3000 in June, bringing other crypto assets with it – but this price was difficult to realise, as many exchanges had trouble sending out hard currency at all.

## Bitfinex: the hack, the bank block and the second bubble

Taiwan-based Bitfinex is one of the more popular Bitcoin exchanges. Advocates like and trust it and enjoy using it – it has margin trading and other fancy features, and lists a wide variety of crypto assets – and recommend it to others.

Bitfinex was originally based on a leaked[228] copy of the codebase from defunct exchange Bitcoinica, which was founded by sixteen-year-old Bitcointalk user "Zhoutong" and shut down after being hacked in 2012. Its software turned out to be made entirely of copy-and-pasted cheese and string that nobody at all knew how to fix. This is quite typical of Bitcoin-related code and systems, as if financial software and systems architecture had never happened. One of Bitfinex's early developers described what the system was like when he had been working on it:[229]

> It has proved impossible to cleanly modularize and upgrade zhoutong's spaghetti code. (Or if it is possible, Bitfinex technical team doesn't know how to proceed.) In the current system, *everything is entangled*. There is no clean separation of concerns. They inherited this steaming shitpile of a codebase and they're stuck with it.
>
> Their legacy data model, as implemented in their current system is insane. The system was *designed by a 16 year old* FFS! Everything is ad hoc, there is no specification, there was zero documentation, there is minimal accounting for edge cases, exception handling was tacked on as an afterthought. There

was no thinking things through. *Everything is ad-hoc!* Therefore it kinda works except when it doesn't!

A Bitfinex representative responded stating that "a grand total of 0 lines from Bitcoinica's code exist on Bitfinex" – the site moved at least partially to the AlphaPoint platform in 2015[230] – but the developer asked him to explain, if Bitfinex had an all-new codebase, how they had accurately reproduced bugs that dated back to Bitcoinica.[231]

The software problems were glossed over for years, because day traders are otherwise known as compulsive gamblers, and crypto day traders make foreign exchange day traders look sober, considered and balanced. The traders didn't care as long as it mostly worked and they could keep trading. And, to be fair, the traders *loved* the Bitfinex platform. Bitfinex worked to polish up its front-end usability and back-end system software, and prided itself on its quality as a crypto trading platform.

Then, on 2 August 2016, nearly 120,000 BTC (then around US$68 million) was stolen from Bitfinex customer accounts.

Bitfinex had set up customers' funds each in their own individual segregated wallet with three keys: one held by Bitfinex, one held by third-party agency BitGo and one held by either the user or Bitfinex (as an offline backup key). BitGo had built an API for Bitfinex to manage this. Any transfer would require two of the three keys.[232] Their aim was to provide greater transparency, with transactions visible on the blockchain, and it also hampered attempts to use the exchange as a mixer.

Bitfinex would send transactions to BitGo, who would check the transaction was in accord with the policy set for that wallet, and sign if it was. BitGo's API allowed policy changes – but it included unintended functionality allowing *global* limits to be changed, without explicit out-of-band confirmation. Neither Bitfinex nor BitGo had realised this vulnerability – but the hacker did.

Full details of the hack have yet to be released. But it appears the hacker knew both Bitfinex and BitGo's systems intimately. They got into Bitfinex's system, gained access to the accounts that could change limits and sent a global limit change, thus allowing them to proceed to withdraw thousands of Bitcoins.

Usually a theft of this magnitude heralds an exchange disappearing or shutting up shop with apologies, or local regulators noticing its existence and swooping in. Bitfinex considered going into bankruptcy, which might leave customers waiting years for a payout. But as the supplier of ~~gambling~~ trading facilities not available elsewhere, Bitfinex felt there was sufficient demand for their services that a drastic action would be considered acceptable to their users: rather than have some customers take a 100% loss, they assessed a 36% "haircut" on all customer deposits – including non-Bitcoin deposits. Depositors whose coins had been hacked would be compensated with money from depositors who hadn't: "we are leaning towards a socialized loss scenario among bitcoin balances and active loans to BTCUSD positions."[233] The company would then try to trade its way out.

You might think that compensating your customers using money from other customers, while the owners don't take a hit, would be against the rules in any reasonable financial system. Particularly as bankruptcies usually pay depositors and creditors first and equity holders last. But welcome to Bitcoin.

Why on earth did the users put up with this? Secondly, because this was claimed to be the haircut they'd take if Bitfinex were to liquidate.[234] (Bitfinex didn't show their working.) But firstly, because they were desperate for continued access to their favoured strip mall casino. Bitfinex promptly went back up to No. 1 on the Bitcoin exchange volume charts.

(Some users did consider suing, but found the company "a Matryoshka doll of shady shell companies in different jurisdictions, so it's hard to work out what the right place to sue them is. Then you have the cost and time of the lawsuit, and if the tokens aren't worth much by the time you get to the end of this long and expensive process there's a risk they'll go into liquidation anyhow."[235])

Bitfinex didn't want its users to feel they'd been left high and dry. So it offered them Bitfinex tokens (BFX) for their losses, saying that they'd come through at some later date on these IOUs and reimburse the holders with their face value:[236]

> The token is a notional credit, is dependent on the Bitfinex Group's recovery of Losses, and is subordinated to any claims against the Bitfinex Group not related to the Losses.

You could even trade these tokens – trading away your right to reimbursement if the stolen coins were recovered – and use them as collateral for margin trading.[237] Though only on Bitfinex:

> The token and your rights pursuant thereto may not be assigned except with notice to, and the prior consent of, the

Bitfinex Group, on terms to be determined by the Bitfinex Group.

You might think this would constitute offering an unregistered security, but welcome to Bitcoin. The price for BFX dropped below its $1 face value even before release, opening at $0.80 and ending the day at $0.32.

Bitfinex redeemed about 1% of the BFX in early September. As it happened, they had enabled margin trading on BFX itself one day before, and the price went up from $0.40 to $0.56 just *before* the announcement.

Around the time of the 1% redemption, 30% of trading on Bitfinex was BFX, which they collected trading fees on. The BFX tokens also kept their customers on Bitfinex in the hope of a payout, rather than just cashing out and never coming back.

In late September, they offered conversion of BFX into equity in their company, iFinex Inc.[238] In October, they came up with another layer: the Recovery Right Token (RRT), for everyone who had sold their BFX for equity.[239] Should any of the stolen coins ever be recovered, Bitfinex would first pay back the BFX holders who had not converted their BFX to something else, then pay back RRT holders with the remainder. That's a token on a token on money they would normally have had to pay back. You could also trade the RRTs on the exchange.[240]

Convoluted arrangements like this are part of why bankruptcy laws, let alone financial trading regulations, exist: so that creditors and depositors get paid first and fairly in a clear and open manner.

In the meantime, Bitfinex promised a financial and security audit. Not by any such tawdry profession as actual *accountants*; they were going to use "Ledger Labs Inc., a top blockchain forensics and technology firm," which happens to be run by Vitalik Buterin, creator of Ethereum (of which more later).[241] They later admitted this audit had never happened.[242]

Bitfinex then posted an open letter to the hacker, seeking "a mutually agreeable arrangement in exchange for an enormous bug bounty", *i.e.,* if only they would explain how they'd hacked Bitfinex: "Our interest here is not to accuse, blame or make demands, but rather to discuss an arrangement that we think you will find interesting."[243]

It was entirely unclear to any observer what possible arrangement could be more interesting to the thief than "I have all your bitcoins now." The stolen bitcoins are slowly being sold off through other exchanges,[244] which is very like a bank accepting a big bag of dye-marked notes known to have been robbed from another bank and deciding they don't care.

On 3 April 2017, Bitfinex announced they would finally redeem the other 99% of the BFX tokens for their $1.00 face value![245] They paid back the dollar value of the stolen bitcoins at the time of the theft – *i.e.,* about half what it was by April. Their haircut gamble had paid off, and they were proud to have made their users whole once more: "We've demonstrated an alternative to bankruptcy."[246]

What they didn't announce was that in mid-March, Wells Fargo had told Bitfinex's Taiwanese banks that it would stop accepting international US dollar wires from Bitfinex, cutting them off entirely as of 31 March. The BFX token redemption was only a number in the user's USD account on Bitfinex, and not anything that could be withdrawn. (Some larger customers could get US dollars out to a limited degree,[247] but as I write this in June 2017, retail customers still can't reliably get US dollars out.)

Banking relationships are a perennial problem for crypto exchanges – banks, and particularly correspondent banks (whose customers are other banks), hate dealing with money service businesses because the KYC/AML compliance is complicated and expensive. Phil Potter, Chief Strategy Officer, noted on a Bitcoin podcast during the Wells Fargo problems:[248]

> We've had banking hiccups in the past, we've just always been able to route around it or deal with it, open up new accounts, or what have you ... shift to a new corporate entity, lots of cat and mouse tricks.

Bitfinex filed suit against Wells Fargo on 5 April, stating that their business was now "crippled" and under "existential threat" and seeking a temporary restraining order.[249] They still hadn't told their customers there was any problem, though users had been reporting withdrawal problems since mid-March. They dropped the suit on 12 April,[250] at that stage having only admitted the problem to customers already discussing it on Reddit.

(Mark Karpelès noted how when Mt. Gox was cut off by its US bank, his lawyers advised that suing the intermediate bank was "the worst thing we could possibly do" and "the best way to see yourself blocked from all banks."[251])

On 18 April, Bitfinex's Taiwanese banks also stopped incoming wires.[252] By 20 April, no international withdrawals were possible in any currency, only domestic withdrawals within Taiwan.[253]

All these fresh US dollars returned to BFX token holders then caused the price of a bitcoin to go *up*, which ended up launching the second great Bitcoin bubble – from $900 per bitcoin at the start of April to $1900 in mid-May and $3000 in early June.[254] The mechanism is:

1. Users have a USD account and a BTC account. They can't sell their bitcoins and withdraw their cash, but they can buy more bitcoins using their newly-topped-up USD account – which contains trapped "dollars" which can't be used for anything else. Think of it as a Bitfinex "USD" token, not as actual US dollars – Disneyland fun-money which can only be spent inside the theme park. The price goes up. In April, BTC on Bitfinex was often $200 higher than elsewhere.

2. With the higher price on Bitfinex, traders arbitrage by buying coins on an exchange with a lower price and selling them on Bitfinex. (Note that the USD from the sale is stuck on Bitfinex.) This raises the price on the other exchanges.

3. Expectations rise, the price gets mainstream press and more people get into Bitcoin. The bubble inflates.

This works precisely *because* you can't get your money out – and other exchanges were also having problems with US dollar withdrawals. Users were reluctant to remove their BTC from Bitfinex because the "price" was highest there (even if unrealisable) and because they loved it as a trading platform.

The trapped "USD" also gets used to buy other cryptocurrencies – the price of altcoins tends to rise and fall with the price of bitcoins – and this has fueled new ICOs ("Initial Coin Offerings," detailed next chapter), as people desperately look for somewhere to put their unspendable "dollars." This got Ethereum and ICOs into the bubble as well.

Even better: on Bitfinex, you can use BTC as collateral to margin-trade on USD, which you can then use to buy more BTC. Which also drives the price up.[255] And, of course, you can't get the USD out, so you might as well buy more cryptos with it.

(Bitfinex certainly didn't intend to start a bubble, and Bitcoin is prone to wild swings of speculation anyway; as I write this, BTC is actually *lower* at Bitfinex than at other exchanges. The bubble continues.)

While it's good for Bitfinex's customers that the company's desperate gamble paid off, it was a desperate gamble. One problem is that others seem to have taken it as a model. South Korean exchange Yapizon was hacked on 22 April, with 3,816 BTC (then about $5 million) being stolen. It too has applied a 37% haircut – coincidentally about the same percentage that Bitfinex applied – to all customer BTC accounts, in exchange for a token called Fei.[256]

Although Bitfinex has considerably professionalised since then, the original founder of Bitfinex, Raphael Nicolle, never seemed to appreciate the problem financial regulators tend to have with schemes that pay early investors using money from later investors. He enthusiastically backed the Pirateat40 Ponzi – though at least he later apologised for that one[257] – and came up with a high-yield scheme of his own:

> So I'm thinking of the following plan: when I need more coins than I have to fill an order, I will ask everyone that previously "registered" with me to lend me some btc. After 7 days, I will return all of it, principal + 2% interests. For you to be contacted, you would have to post here or in PM to say you might lend me bitcoins, and approx. how many you'd be willing to lend me.[258]

Nicolle has not been seen online since the 120,000 BTC hack.[259]

Bitfinex does answer one common question asked of Bitcoin sceptics:

"If you're so critical of Bitcoin, why don't you short it?"

*"Well ..."*

# Chapter 9: Altcoins

Bitcoin was an open protocol implemented in open source code. So alternate cryptocurrencies, or *altcoins*, quickly sprang up – mostly slightly-tweaked versions of the Bitcoin code, many generated automatically at the now-defunct service coingen.io.

Other blockchains might have different hashes, block sizes, block times or consensus models (how to choose who adds the next block). Short times mean you can verify transactions faster, but too short a time means a block may not get all the way across the network before it's time for the next block – leading to "confirmed" transactions no longer being confirmed when another version of that blockchain is found that's longer.

Proof of Work is obviously wasteful. The other main proposed consensus model is Proof of Stake, in which the next block miner is chosen at random according to how many coins they already own. This saves on wasted hashing, but is a bit too blatantly a rentier economy – "thems what has, gets." And, like every other economic endeavour in history, it will obviously tend toward people putting in up to $50 worth of effort to acquire $50 worth of coins – a stealth "proof of work" however you try to structure it. (Although it may be less ecologically destructive – spending $49.99 of your bank balance generates less carbon dioxide than burning $49.99 worth of coal.)

A few altcoins have tried new ideas, such as Namecoin (an attempt to implement an alternate Internet DNS system on a blockchain), Freicoin (which uses demurrage – negative interest – to discourage speculative hoarding) and Curecoin and Foldingcoin (whose Proof of Work is protein folding for Folding@Home, a distributed computing project for disease research). But most have a much simpler value proposition: you might get rich too if you start your own magical Internet money!

The usual scheme is that the creators have more of the coin than anyone else, substantially pre-mining the coin before release. They launch it with speculative promises of interesting future features, then sell their coin off (for bitcoins), telling the new bagholders they're actually early adopters. Some went further: DafuqCoin compromised exchanges with a rootkit because the exchanges failed to check the code before running it.[260] [261]

Bitcoin advocates correctly consider most altcoins a scam and can effortlessly list all the problems with them – while failing to note that most of these are also problems with the substantially early-adopter-owned Bitcoin.

Cryptocurrency advocates and lazy journalists like to talk about the "market cap" of a crypto, which is the total number of coins or tokens in existence multiplied by today's price. This is a bogus number that's not actually applicable to anything – it's not money that was put into the crypto, it's not a realisable value like a company market cap, it doesn't affect prices – it's just an easily-calculated number that sounds good in a headline. Trading is so thin in any crypto, even Bitcoin, that you could never realise a fraction of the number. If you want to compare interest and activity in crypto assets, you need to compare trading volumes, if you can find good numbers for those.

## Litecoin

Litecoin is the "me too" coin. It hasn't many interesting stories, but it was the most prominent altcoin before the first Bitcoin bubble burst; for a few years, sites like the Pirate Bay that accepted Bitcoin donations often also accepted Litecoin donations. It was marketed as "the silver to Bitcoin's gold." The main difference from Bitcoin is a different hash designed to be resistant to GPU mining (though ASICs eventually came out) and a shorter block time.

Litecoin's price went up with Bitcoin's until 2013, the price crashed with Bitcoin's, and during 2014 it declined from its peak of $42 (spot prices of $68 on some exchanges) to $1.50. It hovered around $4 until it hit $30 in the second bubble – altcoin prices tend to track Bitcoin's price – and the small current volume is Chinese speculators.

## Dogecoin

Dogecoin (pronounced "dozhe-coin" or "dogue-coin") started in December 2013, originally as a joke based on the "Doge" Shiba Inu Internet meme. The idea was mostly to have some fun with cryptocurrency cheap enough to mess around with; and who knows, maybe we'll all get rich!

Dogecoiners ("shibes"), gathering on Reddit /r/dogecoin, still dreamt of a cryptocurrency payday – but they made an explicit point of being nicer as a community than Bitcoin advocates, who had quite a reputation by this stage.

Dogecoin got caught up in the hype of the Bitcoin bubble and quickly gained in price, peaking in January 2014 at 0.17 of a cent per DOGE, despite almost no use cases (some used it to tip other Reddit commenters) and not being exchangeable for anything but bitcoins. The Dogecoin Foundation, started by Ben Doernberg and the coin's creator Jackson Palmer, raised nearly $30,000 of Dogecoins in January to send the Jamaican bobsled team to the 2014 Winter Olympics. Doge4Water raised $32,000 for clean water in Kenya.

This attracted the attention of a fellow calling himself Alex Green. "My name is Alex Green. I have zero online footprint." He quickly set up UK cryptocurrency exchange Moolah. While others tipped single Dogecoins, worth a fraction of a penny, Green caught attention with tips of thousands of dollars.

Dogecoin then raised $50,000 to sponsor a NASCAR racer, Josh Wise. (Green put in $15,000 himself.) Wise's race in May 2014 was probably the media peak for Dogecoin.

Green started fundraisers on /r/dogecoin for shares in Moolah, and never mind those fiddly regulations about promoting securities to the general public. By mid-June, he had raised over half a million dollars. He had also pushed most of the original Dogecoin crowd into leaving, repeatedly threatening to sue Palmer and Doernberg for harassment for questioning his use of /r/dogecoin to push unregistered securities.

Palmer and Doernberg correctly smelt a rat. It came out that "Green" was formerly known as Ryan Kennedy, Ryan Gentle, Ryan Francis and multiple other names, with a long history of creating scam startups that raised funds and then vanished.[262] Moolah shut down in October and "Green" disappeared with the money.

Moolah had taken over cryptocurrency exchange Mintpal in July 2014. That exchange shut down with Moolah in October after a "hack". Kennedy was caught selling the Mintpal bitcoins on LocalBitcoins in February 2015.[263]

As well as a serial scammer, Kennedy turned out to be a serial rapist, convicted in May 2016 of three counts of rape[264] and jailed for 11 years. He was also charged over the stolen Mintpal bitcoins in June 2017.[265]

With Green/Kennedy no longer in the picture, /r/dogecoin recovered its spirit somewhat, refused to worry about prices any more and is back to just having fun, though with wistful dreams of crypto riches. Unlike other cryptocurrencies' claims about their prices, Dogecoin may succeed in going "to the moon!" – the community sponsored sending a physical Dogecoin on an Astrobotic commercial moon shot.[266]

It came out in May 2017 that the operator of the Dogecoin tipping bot on Reddit had stolen all the deposited Dogecoins two years earlier.[267] Much sorry, many loss.

# Ethereum

Ethereum was proposed by Vitalik Buterin (an early Bitcoiner and a co-founder of *Bitcoin Magazine*) and developed by Buterin, Gavin Wood, Jeffrey Wilcke and others. Its key innovation is that you can run *smart contracts* on a blockchain: programs that are triggered to run automatically in a given circumstance. If Bitcoin is like an Excel spreadsheet, then Ethereum is like a spreadsheet with macros. This new idea was interesting enough to quickly make Ethereum the second most popular cryptocurrency.

Transactions and smart contract programs (which they call "dapps," short for "distributed applications") require *gas* (a certain amount of the currency token, *ether*, abbreviated ETH), which is paid to the miner whose computer runs the transaction or smart contract. This also keeps smart contracts from running forever.

Ethereum has its own home-brewed Proof of Work hash[268] which is designed to be ASIC-resistant, to avoid mining centralisation – it requires a few gigabytes of fast memory on hand, so mining is presently GPU-based. There are loose plans to move to Proof of Stake.[269] (For a while during the second crypto bubble, you could actually make money mining ether on last year's video card, which led to a small gold rush in the video cards themselves,[270] and an ensuing glut of burnt-out cards on the second-hand market.)

Ethereum's pitch has always been ridiculously aspirational. It's a "smart contracts platform," it's a "worldwide distributed computer," at one point Wikipedia called it "Web 3.0," at another a "publishing platform." Anything other than a *cryptocurrency*. To this day, drive-by editors occasionally swing by the Ethereum article in Wikipedia to remove the word "cryptocurrency."

Of course, the cryptocurrency is overwhelmingly the main use, and that the cryptocurrency will go to the moon is the main hope.

Ethereum has a block time of around 14 to 16 seconds (Bitcoin's is 10 minutes). How do blocks make it across the network in that time? Well, often they don't (though blocks only being a few kilobytes helps[271]). So there are about 7% valid but orphaned blocks.[272] A miner can store up to two failed blocks in their block as "uncles," and the miners of the blocks that became uncles get some reward too; Ethereum picks the highest-scoring chain, and uncles give a block a higher score. This avoids penalising miners who are further away from the rest of the network, reducing economic pressure to centralise. The unconfirmed transactions in the uncle will usually stay around until they finally make it into a block. The existence of a single canonical blockchain is frequently questionable, but somehow it all muddles forth.

Ethereum has a current maximum of about 14 transactions per second[*] (Bitcoin's is 7 TPS). As at mid-2017 it's running about 2-3 TPS, having rapidly risen over 2017;[273] popular dapps already fill the blocks and clog the system for hours at a time, such as the Bancor and Status ICOs. The Ethereum community seems to have faith in the Ethereum Foundation, so a fix is more likely to be accepted without a Bitcoin-style community civil war; and backward-compatibility-breaking changes in Ethereum are a regular occurrence and are *mostly* managed without controversy.

The developers have always stated that Ethereum is explicitly experimental and unfinished (and never mind the hundreds of millions of dollars in ether swilling around in it), and that the promised fancy functionality will need years of work.[274] They occasionally boggle at people treating it as much more of a finished product than they do.[275]

Ethereum advocates talk up corporate adoption by Microsoft and other companies – it's a popular choice of platform for business blockchain trials, and its smart contract functionality is reused by a lot of other blockchain software – but this is adoption of the software to

---

[*]     1 "gas" is 0.00001 ETH. Transaction throughput will be gas limit divided by block time, divided by 21,000 for a single transaction. The gas limit is variable, but is currently around 4,7000,000. So 4,700,000/16 seconds/21,000 = 13.99 transactions per second.

run separate in-house blockchains, not adoption of the public Ethereum chain and currency.

## Buterin's quantum quest

Before Ethereum, Vitalik Buterin put considerable effort in 2013 into trying to convince investors to fund him to build a quantum computer. (Note that no quantum computers able to solve practical problems are verified as existing as of early 2017.) His plan was to use this quantum computer to solve computationally infeasible problems that can't be done practically on an ordinary computer, such as reversing cryptographic hash functions.[276]

Since he didn't know how to build a quantum computer, his plan was to *simulate* one on an ordinary computer – since this apparently wouldn't count as just running a program to solve the impossible problem. This was an idea that had long been put forward by Jordan Ash, his associate in this endeavour, who had put considerable effort into this startlingly crank mathematical notion.[277]

Buterin and Ash's plan was to use this simulated quantum computer not to revolutionise computation and change the world – but only to use it to mine bitcoins faster than anyone else and corner the market.

Sadly for their Fields Medal hopes, they failed to secure sufficient funding to break mathematics. Investors may have been put off by the pointed questions from the crowd on how, quite apart from the mathematical implausibility, this would destroy any confidence in Bitcoin and kill the golden goose.

It's worth noting that a practical quantum computer would be able to solve the SHA-256 hash used in Bitcoin somewhat faster than an ordinary computer* – but it could also quickly break the conventionally-unbreakable public-key encryption that protects a user's Bitcoin balance. So if you secretly had a quantum computer, you could mine a bit faster, *or* you could just steal everyone else's bitcoins.

Buterin later said he had "greatly overestimated" the likelihood of the team breaking mathematics, estimating this task at maybe 1% to 5% possible (apparently a purely subjective guess, with no basis or

---

\*   $O(\sqrt{N})$ rather than $O(N)$, per Grover's algorithm. Which is a pretty good speedup for as long as nobody else knows you have a quantum computer.

working given for this number), and assures us that his skepticism concerning quantum claims has "substantially increased." He now puts the probability at "<0.1%", though competent observers would likely consider even that on the high side for a mathematical impossibility.[278]

# ICOs: magic beans and bubble machines

> There is nothing in the world more helpless and irresponsible and depraved than a man in the depths of an ether binge.
>
> – Hunter S. Thompson, *Fear and Loathing in Las Vegas*

The snappy new phrase for "buy our premined altcoin" is "ICO" ("Initial Coin Offering" or "Initial Crowdfunding Offering"). These are typically tokens running on top of the Ethereum blockchain, usually in a smart contract written to the standard ERC-20 interface.[279]

There's no mining involved – you create a smart contract that manages a pile of tokens, sell a small percentage and hold the rest to sell later. You also keep centralised control over the token. If it's ERC-20 compliant, it's easy for an exchange to trade in it.

An ICO makes sense for crowdfunding in very limited conditions – if you have a technical problem that requires decentralised, cryptographically verified tokens (if it doesn't need tokens, they shouldn't be bolted on); if the tokens are directly usable on the platform itself; if at least a proof-of-concept of the technology verifiably exists. It also helps if the idea is even plausible as a business. Unsurprisingly, most ICOs don't meet these criteria.

Token offerings have been around a while, but kicked off enormously in the second bubble. The usual pretext is crowdfunding, but in practice the tokens are just traded on the exchanges as commodities. The creators then cash in. The value proposition for buyers is, as for the creators, easy money in a bubble.

Bancor's ICO raised $144 million with none of the due diligence of an ordinary Initial Public Offering, the barest prospectus and no indication their plan (a "market maker" to sell altcoins that aren't selling otherwise) would even work. This is clearly superior, for a certain type of seller, to the IPO bubble of the dot-com era, in that these aren't actually shares, and the purchasers have no influence over the funded enterprise even in theory.

The ideas themselves are as bad as the worst dot-com IPOs. Digix, the first token crowdsale on the Ethereum blockchain itself, is a cryptocurrency backed by gold;[280] Golem offers a "decentralized" (buzzword alert!) market in computing, like Amazon Web Services except you can only pay using their token;[281] Gnosis offers semiautomatic prediction markets using their token;[282] SingularDTV is a bizarre plan to fund a TV show about the Singularity in which a Caribbean island adopts Ethereum as its currency and Austrian economics works (this one gets its own section later in the book); Iconomi is an index fund of other ICOs.[283]

The token smart contracts are often incompetent in both intended functionality and programming ability.[284] This turns out not to matter as long as they do the basic job: attract buyers and sell tokens. Status raised 300,000 ETH (then over $100 million) to … write an Ethereum phone app. Hopefully that's enough to develop a phone app! It sold out in just a few hours. The actual promises as to what people will get for that $100 million are typical:[285]

> **Risk of abandonment / lack of success** : The User understands and accepts that the creation of the SNT and the development of the Status Project may be abandoned for a number of reasons, including lack of interest from the public, lack of funding, lack of commercial success or prospects (e.g. caused by competing projects). The User therefore understands that there is no assurance that, even if the Status Project is partially or fully developed and launched, the User will receive any benefits through the SNT held by him.

EOS, founded by serial blockchain entrepreneur Danny Larimer, is as direct as possible in this regard. They're also marketing it to the general public, with advertisements on the sides of London taxis.[286] Here's how the white paper describes it:[287]

> The EOS.IO software introduces a new blockchain architecture designed to enable vertical and horizontal scaling of decentralized applications. This is achieved by creating an operating system-like construct upon which applications can be built. The software provides accounts, authentication, databases, asynchronous communication and the scheduling of applications across hundreds of CPU cores or clusters. The resulting technology is a blockchain architecture that scales to

millions of transactions per second, eliminates user fees, and allows for quick and easy deployment of decentralized applications.

No, that doesn't end "and a pony." EOS is a rebranding of Larimer's 2014 project BitShares,[288] which failed to achieve this either.

EOS is releasing *one billion* tokens, in daily tranches over the course of a year, at a price of "how much money do you have to throw at us?" Really, that's the price: the day's take in ETH divided by the number of tokens released that day.

So I send in some ether, and I get ...[289]

> The EOS Tokens do not have any rights, uses, purpose, attributes, functionalities or features, express or implied, including, without limitation, any uses, purpose, attributes, functionalities or features on the EOS Platform.

The legal EOS Token Purchase Agreement is a frankly amazing document that everyone should read.[290] US citizens or residents are not to buy the tokens (though EOS assures us they totally don't constitute a security – hear that, SEC?); the tokens are defined as not being useful in any manner whatsoever; forty-eight hours after the end of the distribution period, the tokens will no longer be transferable; the buyer promises not to purchase them for speculation or investment. If there's any legal problems caused by you buying these officially worthless things, you agree to indemnify EOS.

Crypto fans *still lined up to buy them.* "Whatever these people do, I'm going all in. Nuff said."[291]

EOS was also driven up by another ICO, press.one, a "Content Distribution Public Chain" to run on the forthcoming EOS blockchain.[292] The press.one ICO sells 20% of its tokens for bitcoins, 30% for ether and 50% for EOS tokens. Founder Xiaolai Li is an EOS/BitShares investor.

Chinese speculators went all-in on ICOs, buying into dubious proposals from fear of missing out, to the point where exchange BTC38 refused to put new tokens up and warned that illicit fundraising can carry the death penalty in China.[293] One Chinese "ICO" broke new barriers in market efficiency: you didn't even need to put your ether into it yourself! Because the "white paper" contained malware that found your Ethereum wallet and emptied it. Now that's a *smart* contract.[294]

The other big problem with ICOs is that they're already recreating the Bitcoin transaction clog, but on Ethereum. Both the Bancor and Status ICOs filled the blocks on the day of their release, with Status's higher transaction fees blocking all smaller transaction fees for several hours. Some exchanges had to stop trading ETH because they couldn't get transactions onto the Ethereum blockchain.[295]

History doesn't repeat, but it does rhyme. One of the most famous share offerings from the South Sea Bubble of 1719-1720 was "A company for carrying on an undertaking of great advantage, but nobody to know what it is":[296]

> The man of genius who essayed this bold and successful inroad upon public credulity, merely stated in his prospectus that the required capital was half a million, in five thousand shares of 100 pounds each, deposit 2 pounds per share. Each subscriber, paying his deposit, would be entitled to 100 pounds per annum per share. How this immense profit was to be obtained, he did not condescend to inform them at that time, but promised that in a month full particulars should be duly announced, and a call made for the remaining 98 pounds of the subscription. Next morning, at nine o'clock, this great man opened an office in Cornhill. Crowds of people beset his door, and when he shut up at three o'clock, he found that no less than one thousand shares had been subscribed for, and the deposits paid. He was thus, in five hours, the winner of 2000 pounds. He was philosopher enough to be contented with his venture, and set off the same evening for the Continent. He was never heard of again.

The finest ICO remains PonzICO,[297] a piece of "blockchain performance art" wherein earlier contributors are paid directly from later contributors, with the founder taking a meagre 50% off the top. His pitch – "In today's age, it seems better to promote the plausibility of future profit rather than waste energy on actually delivering"[298] – grossed $4000 as of June 2017.[299]

# Chapter 10: Smart contracts, stupid humans

## *Dr. Strangelove*, but on the blockchain

Smart contracts were originally quite separate from cryptocurrencies and blockchains. They were first proposed by Nick Szabo in 1994.[300] You set up a legal agreement in the form of a computer program that triggers when particular conditions are met, and which cannot be interfered with once deployed. The idea is to replace the messy uncertainty and hierarchy of conventional human-mediated legal agreements with the clear, deterministic rigour of computer code, immune to human interference, in order to make business and the law more predictable and effective.

This is a bad idea in every way. Computer code maps very badly to real-world legal agreements, where the hard part is not normal operations, but what to do when things go wrong; immutability means you can't fix problems, programmers need to write perfect bug-free programs first time every time, and the contract can't be updated if circumstances or laws change; if the contract acts on real-world data, that data will often need human interpretation. And imagine your money working as reliably as your PC.

*Dr. Strangelove* is the best-known story of an unstoppable smart contract going wrong, immune to human intervention. The US has sent nuclear bombers to the Soviet Union that can only be recalled with a code that nobody has; if any bombs hit, these will trigger the Soviet Union's deterrent, an unstoppable doomsday device that cannot be dismantled or disarmed, and will explode on any attempt to. The real-life version's consequences are not as drastic, but the misguided thinking is the same.

Fortunately, most of the worst real-world smart contract proposals are infeasible; what they're *actually* used for is "honest Ponzis" and ICO tokens.

## So who wants smart contracts, anyway?

There are five groups of people who want smart contracts:

1. Computer programmers who don't have an aptitude for social or legal conventions, but do have an aptitude for programming, so they'd like social and legal conventions to work a bit more like that.

2. Anarcho-capitalists who want to replace the government with a small DOS batch file. (Particularly ones who are also in the first group.)

3. Businesses who want to automate away dealing with customers, but still take their money.

4. People selling you flim-flam with a thin veneer of technology on top, who have, as we've noted, found rich pickings in smart contracts for ICOs.

5. Innovative entrepreneurs who have come into conflict with the traditional legal system previously, and would like something deterministic enough that they can take your money and escape through the cracks. (See also group 4.)

## Legal code is not computer code

Szabo is a computer scientist who has studied law, and has advocated a role for smart contracts in public law, with due caution.[301] However, others want to take the idea much further.

Some advocates speak of replacing lawyers and judges with computer code,[302] as if this is an obviously good idea; there are even anarcho-capitalists who seriously posit replacing most functions of government with a computer program.[303] Others speak of completely autonomous corporate entities, doing deals with real money and goods without even the possibility of outside interference.[304]

Computer programmers work in an area where everything can be determined cleanly and clearly, if only in principle. So using computers to sort out all those annoying grey areas in human interaction is tempting: if you don't understand law (which involves intent) but you do understand code (which does precisely what you tell it – though maybe not precisely what you meant), then you may try to work around law using code.

The trouble is that this conception of smart contracts is based on a severely limited understanding of how contracts, the law and social agreements work. It concentrates on a technical form that can be put into computer code. It doesn't address the social meaning of what a "contract" is, the changeable contexts real-world contracts operate in, how they're fulfilled in practice – or how you fix them when things go wrong.

With conventional contracts, if there isn't a reasonable human at the wheel, you can in fact go to court. Not all contracts are legally enforceable. In the worst case, a government can pass new law making a severely problematic variety of clause unenforceable.

Smart contracts work on the wrong level: they run on facts and not on human intent – but legal contracts are a codification of human intent. Human intent is inexact, but contracts assume they will be running on human minds in the context of human institutions, for human purposes.

A conventional contract, even one specified as precisely as possible, will have disputes and changes in circumstances, and resolving these will often involve ascertaining what people were thinking at the time and what the world outside the contract was doing. The purpose of law is not to achieve philosophical or mathematical truth, but to take a messy reality and achieve workable results that society can live with.

Even Vitalik Buterin has acknowledged that for smart contracts to work as advertised, we would need to create a human-equivalent artificial intelligence to understand what people *meant* the contract to do[305] – what people were thinking at the time is a key issue in resolving many a contractual dispute. "Intent is fundamentally complex."

## The oracle problem: garbage in, garbage out

In software testing, an *oracle* is any mechanism that determines if a test has passed or failed. The *oracle problem* is how to do this without costly human intervention.

This usage was adopted for smart contracts, where the oracle problem is to determine whether a real-world condition in a smart contract has been met.

Unless you just want to shuffle tokens inside your smart contract platform, at some point you're going to need to interact with the outside world. Your contract has to know if a shipment has not just been delivered but is what you ordered, or if a given piece of work has been done to a satisfactory standard. This will frequently involve unavoidable trust in human judgement.

And remember: garbage in means garbage out. You may set up incentives against false data – but what about accidental errors, or disputed data, or unavailable data? Or, as Matt Levine from *Bloomberg* points out: "My immutable unforgeable cryptographically secure blockchain record proving that I have 10,000 pounds of aluminum in a warehouse is not much use to a bank if I then smuggle the aluminum out of the warehouse through the back door."[306]

Technology and business journalists writing about non-cryptocurrency use cases for smart contracts never seem to mention that their "trustless" system will still involve trusting humans wherever it touches the physical world. You may have a tamperproof system for running contract code, but the inputs have to come from outside this secure space.

A common proposal is to outsource your oracle to a prediction market – humans betting on predictions – that is also on your blockchain, such as Augur. Somehow, the outcome of a bet is supposed to substitute for direct knowledge of an event having happened or not, with sufficient confidence in the process to let it affect your money. If your question isn't popular enough to attract sufficient uninvolved wagers – it would often be worth it for one party to just bribe the bettors – you will still have the oracle problem in determining whether the event has in fact occurred. You can't get rid of the human element by adding another layer of indirection – it's oracles all the way down.

(Augur has openly bragged that they think running on a blockchain means they can dodge US government regulation on gambling and derivatives, which led to the shutdown of previous prediction markets, despite being a single company with known principals.[307])

# Immutability: make your mistakes unfixable

The value proposition of "immutability" is that nobody can mess with your contract once it's been deployed. The common pitch to musicians, for example, is that the big record label will *have* to pay you as it says in your contract, quickly and automatically.

But in practice, immunity to human interference is as serious a problem as Bitcoin transactions being irreversible. The *standard* example of a real-world smart contract is a car that stops working if your payment fails.[308] Or its Internet connection fails. Or there's a software bug. Unstoppably, immune to human intercession or changes in circumstances.

In the real world, circumstances change out from under you. How many musicians have been so pleased with the first contract they signed, and understood it themselves so well, that they'd never want one dot of it altered? Including by, say, later court proceedings.

The most famous attempt at an autonomous corporation immune to interference, The DAO, crashed and burned when it turned out to have a security hole that couldn't be fixed in time and got hacked, as detailed later in this chapter.

The eventual fix for The DAO hack demonstrates the other problem with smart contracts: the "immutable" system containing the smart contract was suddenly considered changeable the moment the big boys risked losing enough money.

(Szabo's original 1994 paper noted the need to allow human intervention, though by 2014 he was fully into smart contracts on a blockchain with no human intervention possible.[309] He didn't offer any comment on the 2016 failure of The DAO.)

# Immutability: the enemy of good software engineering

Smart contracts make no sense as software engineering. You need a perfect bug-free program – but humans are *really* bad at coding without error. Programming to this extreme quality level is done by organisations like NASA for spacecraft, and it's hideously slow and expensive. (Everyday businesses would find a floor full of lawyers both cheaper and more effective.)

A much-touted advantage of smart contracts is that the code is public, so anyone can check and verify it before engaging with it. The problem is that it is extremely difficult to tell precisely what a program might possibly do without actually running it.* Even if you do see any obvious (or exploitable) bugs, nobody can fix them once the contract's been deployed – your bugs are immutable.

Then there's the question of what's an error and what's deliberate. In the wider world of security programming, we have the Underhanded C Contest, a competition to write deceptive programs that look like they just have a bug: "you must write C code that is as readable, clear, innocent and straightforward as possible, and yet it must fail to perform at its apparent function. To be more specific, it should perform some specific underhanded task that will not be detected by examining the source code." The Ethereum community is also running one for Solidity, to encourage security awareness. If you think people have trouble with loopholes and traps in conventional contracts …

Smart contracts rely on the program being perfect and not having any bugs. But they also rely on the *language* (*e.g.*, Solidity in Ethereum) being perfect and not having any bugs. And the *platform the language runs on* (*e.g.*, the Ethereum Virtual Machine) being perfect and not having any bugs. You can deploy fully-audited code that you've mathematically proven is correct – and then a bug in a lower layer means you have a security hole anyway. And this has already happened.[310]

## Ethereum smart contracts in practice

> If you suspect that spending crypto-currencies on virtual thrones for non-existent kingdoms is illegal in your jurisdiction, please avoid participating (and complain to your political representatives).
>
> – chain-letter automatic Ponzi scheme "King of the Ether"[311]

For decades, smart contracts were just an interesting hypothetical. When blockchains came along, smart contract advocates were very interested in the blockchain's immutability. There were some smart

---

\* For instance, the famous Shellshock exploit was in completely open and widely-used code, but wasn't noticed until 25 *years* after the bug had been introduced.

contract experiments on Bitcoin, but Ethereum was pretty much the first practical platform for writing and running computer programs on a blockchain.

Humans are bad at tasks requiring perfection. But when programming errors have drastic consequences, the usual approach is to make it harder to shoot yourself in the foot: functional programming languages, formal methods, mathematical verification of the code, don't use a full computer language (avoid Turing completeness), and so on. Szabo wrote up some requirements and a simple example language in 2002.[312]

This is particularly important when you have multiple smart contracts interacting with each other – massively concurrent programming, with unknown possibly-hostile programs calling into functions of yours.

Ethereum ignores all of this. Its standard contract language, Solidity, is a procedural language based on the web programming language JavaScript – to make it as easy as possible for beginners to write their first smart contract. It contains many constructs that mislead programmers coming from JavaScript into shooting themselves in the foot.[313] It is ill-suited and hazardous for concurrency (*e.g.,* the Solarstorm vulnerability[314]), despite this being a specific intended use case.

There are endless guides to writing a secure smart contract for Ethereum, but *most* Ethereum contracts ignore them, with the obvious consequences.[315]

Smart contracts on Ethereum are worse than even non-financial commercial code; as of May 2016, Ethereum contracts averaged 100 obvious bugs (so obvious a machine could spot them) per 1000 lines of code.[316] (For comparison, Microsoft code averages 15 obvious bugs per 1000 lines, NASA spacecraft code around 0 per 500,000 lines.)

Since cryptocurrency enthusiasts had already self-selected for gullibility, the very first smart contracts they wrote were chain letters, lotteries and automatic Ponzi schemes. These ably demonstrated the requirement for coding correctly, first time, every time:

- The casino whose pseudorandom number generator had the random seed in the code, so anyone could recreate the precise sequence of random numbers.[317]
- The GovernMental Ponzi was going to pay out 1100 ETH, but due to a coding error this required more gas than the

maximum possible gas for a transaction. The ether is now stuck there forever.[318]

- Many schemes which ran out of gas due to bugs, *e.g.*, King of the Ether.[319]

- Rubixi Ponzi: Errors in the code, copy-and-pasted from other contracts, allowed anyone to become the owner and take the money.[320]

- A Ponzi which would pay out only to the creator of the scheme because of what looked to casual inspection of the code like a typo in a variable name.[321] No doubt just an accident, I'm sure.

Automated Ponzi schemes are not nearly as fashionable in 2017; most of the effort goes into smart contracts for managing ICO tokens. However, as The DAO showed, the coding quality is as good as ever.

# The DAO: the steadfast iron will of unstoppable code

> You just learned chemistry and the first thing you built was a giant bomb and you can't understand why it blew up in your face.
>
> – brockchainbrockshize, /r/ethereum[322]

Not content with their existing sales of Internet fairy gold, some Ethereum developers at German blockchain startup Slock.it came up with an even more complicated scheme: The DAO – a Decentralized Autonomous Organization, with "The" as part of the name. This was a smart contract on Ethereum which would take people's money and give it to projects voted on by the contributors as worth funding: a distributed venture capital firm.

> The DAO's Mission: To blaze a new path in business organization for the betterment of its members, existing simultaneously nowhere and everywhere and operating solely with the steadfast iron will of **unstoppable code**.[323]

Bold in original. I'm sure there are no obvious problems there that jump right out at you.

The DAO launched on 30 April 2016, got massive publicity and became *the biggest crowdfunding in history* up to that time, with over $150 million in ETH from 11,000 investors in DAO tokens. *Fourteen per cent* of all ether was in The DAO. It was the most prominent smart contract of all time, achieving considerable mainstream press coverage. It proceeded to illustrate just about every potential issue that has ever been raised with smart contracts.

The DAO's legal footing was uncertain, and widely questioned. Selling tokens in The DAO closely resembled trading in unregistered securities – particularly when DAO tokens themselves hit cryptocurrency exchanges – and the SEC had come down on similar schemes in the past. There was no corporate entity, so it would default in most legal systems to being a general partnership, with the investors having unlimited personal liability, and the creators and the designated "curators" of the scheme likely also being liable.

Shortly before the go-live date, researchers flagged several mechanisms in the design of The DAO that would almost certainly lead to losses for investors, and called for a moratorium on The DAO until they could be fixed.[324]

Worse, on 9 June a bug was found in multiple smart contracts written in Solidity, including The DAO: if a balance function was called recursively in the right way, you could withdraw money repeatedly at no cost. "Your smart contract is probably vulnerable to being emptied if you keep track of any sort of user balances and were not very, very careful."[325] This was not technically a bug in Solidity, but the language design had made it fatally easy to leave yourself wide open.

The DAO principals decided to proceed anyway, Stephen Tual of Slock.it confidently declaring on 12 June "No DAO funds at risk following the Ethereum smart contract 'recursive call' bug discovery"[326] … and on 17 June, a hacker used this recursive call bug to drain $50 million from The DAO. And nobody could stop this happening, because the smart contract code couldn't be altered without two weeks' consensus from participants. The price of ether promptly dropped from $21.50 to $15.

(Tual posted on 9 July a hopeful list of reasons why the attacker might *give all the ether back*, just like that. Because it would be in their rational self-interest.[327] This didn't happen, oddly enough.)

Ethereum Foundation principals discussed options including a soft fork or a hard fork of the code or even of the blockchain itself, or a rollback of the blockchain. The community wrangled with the philosophical issues: the whole point of smart contracts was that they couldn't be fiddled with. This contract had been advertised as "the steadfast iron will of **unstoppable code**," but it appeared only the hacker had read the contract's fine print closely enough.[*] Some seriously debated whether this should even be regarded as a "theft", saying that code is law and intent doesn't matter (unlike in real-world contracts operating in a legal system, or indeed in fraud law in general). Others argued that the market integrity of the Ethereum smart contract system required that incompetent contracts, which The DAO certainly was, had to be allowed to fail.

(The proposed soft fork solution was to blacklist transactions whose *result* interacted with the "dark DAO" the attacker had poured the funds into. This would have allowed a fairly obvious denial-of-service attack: flood Ethereum with costly computations that end at the dark DAO. In computer science terms, this approach could only have worked by first solving the *halting problem:* you would need to be able to determine the outcome of any possible Ethereum program without actually running it and observing the result.[328])

The DAO was shut down soon after, and on 20 July the Ethereum Foundation – several of whose principals were curators of The DAO[329] and/or heavily invested in it – changed how *the actual code of Ethereum* interpreted their blockchain (the "immutable" ledger) so as to wind back the hack and take back their money. The blockchain was "immutable," so they changed how it was interpreted. The "impossible" bailout had happened.

This illustrated the final major problem with smart contracts: **CODE IS LAW** until the whales are in danger of losing money.

Ethereum promptly split into two separate blockchains, each with its own currency – Ethereum (ETH), the wound-back version, supported by the Ethereum Foundation, and Ethereum Classic (ETC), the original code and blockchain – because all this was too greedy even for crypto fans to put up with. Both blockchains and currencies operate today. Well done, all.

Apologists note that The DAO was just an *experiment* (a $150 million "experiment") to answer the question: can we have a workable decentralized autonomous organization, running on smart contracts, with no human intervention? And it answered it: no, probably not.

---

[*]    There's an amusing (if probably just trolling) open letter purportedly from the attacker, posted to Pastebin, that makes this claim explicitly.

# Chapter 11: Business bafflegab, but on the Blockchain

> If you're a business guy you could look at the current construct versus the new construct and say 'aren't you just building a big database?'
>
> – Charley Cooper, R3 Blockchain Consortium

> You can replace the term "distributed ledgers" with "shared Excel sheets" in about 90 percent of talk about blockchain and finance.
>
> – Tracy Alloway[330]

As Bitcoin became more famous, its dubious nature became increasingly obvious to mainstream observers. So the buzzword of choice shifted from "Bitcoin" to "the blockchain", or just "Blockchain".

They *really* meant the Bitcoin blockchain, as the goal was to get interest up and the price with it. This particularly picked up around late 2014,[331] when the Bitcoin price had cratered. The value proposition was that Bitcoin was the most secure chain as it had the most hashing power, so everyone wanting a blockchain should use that one. However, the limit of 7 transactions per second worldwide, blocks being too full for transactions to get through anyway, and that your Internet of Things light bulb was profoundly unlikely to add enough flash memory for 120 gigabytes of SatoshiDice gambling spam were all a bit too obvious to the prospective customers.

But by late 2015, "Blockchain" hype had taken on a life of its own as a business buzzword. If in a manner somewhat uncomfortable with its Bitcoin origins. This has been further euphemised to "distributed ledger technology," which would on the face of it include shared Excel spreadsheets.

In the real world, nobody outside the cryptocurrency subculture uses blockchains proper, because they are ridiculously impractical and the most prominent one uses as much electricity as all of Ireland. This means their fantasy life is rich indeed.

Repeat to yourself: if it sounds too good to be true, it almost certainly is.

## What can Blockchain do for me?

The key problem with blockchain proposals for business are:

1. Decentralisation is very expensive and doesn't get you much, at the loss of efficiency and control. Recentralising immediately makes the system much more efficient.

2. Your problem is pretty much always sorting out your data and formats, and blockchains won't clean up your data for you.

If you start with "... but with Blockchain!", then putting lots of different words before "but" isn't likely to result in something that's actually useful and practical.

Transaction ledgers in tamper-evident chains and trees of hashes are a good idea, and businesses are about to discover how to use them for tamper-evident ledgers. These will likely be branded "Blockchain," whether or not the product has anything else to do with blockchains.

If you have programmers, they probably save their code in Git, which is the closest I can think of to a useful blockchain-like technology: it saves individual code edits as transactions in Merkle trees with tamper-evident hashes, and developers routinely copy entire Git repositories around, identifying them by hash. It's a distributed ledger, but for computer programs rather than money. What it doesn't have is the blockchain consensus mechanism – you take or leave the version of the repository you're offered. (I have had one "distributed ledger technology" developer admit his product was basically a simplified version of Git.)

Git was released in 2005 and was based on work going back to the late 1990s; Merkle trees were invented in 1979. The good bits of blockchain are not original, and the original bits of blockchain turn out not to be much good. But if you use Git, you can tell your management "oh yes, we've been using *blockchain-related technologies* for years now ..."

Business Blockchain marketing claims are rarely this grounded, however. They're largely divorced from tawdry considerations of technical or economic feasibility, mathematical coherency or logical consistency. Normal people hear these nigh-magical claims, see obvious uses for them in their own business and are left with the impression "Blockchain" can get them these things.

Some of the claims are sort of true in some sense, but most are completely fanciful. Many start from a hypothetical use case – often lifted directly from the wildest Bitcoin advocacy – then tout the hypothetical as if it were an existing and practical technology. This includes claims made for "distributed ledger technology," which also mostly originate in Bitcoin advocacy.[332]

IBM's promotional e-book *Making Blockchain Ready for Business*[333] is a good example. It sells vague and implied future potential – "discover what new business models could emerge if trust & manual processes are eliminated"; "how might a faster, more secure, standardized, and operationally efficient transaction model create new opportunities for your business?" Almost every solid-looking "is" statement concerning blockchains – "an enterprise-class, cross-industry open standard for distributed ledgers that can transform the way business transactions are conducted globally"; "highly secure blockchain services and frameworks that address regulatory compliance across financial services, government, and healthcare" – is really a "might" or "could"; no blockchain has all the claimed abilities in the present day, and certainly not Hyperledger, the basis of IBM Blockchain.

I sat in on one presentation by a Big Four accounting firm on the Blockchain in health care: three blokes (one with a tie, two without) talking about the hypothetical *possibilities* a blockchain might offer health care in the future, all of which was generic extruded blockchain hype, and much of it Bitcoin hype with the buzzword changed. When an audience member, tiring of this foggy talk, asked if there was anything *concrete* that blockchains could offer the NHS, they responded that asking for practical uses of Blockchain was "like trying to predict Facebook in 1993." The main takeaway for the health care sector people I was with was swearing never to use said accounting firm for anything whatsoever that wasn't accounting.

A sure tell of a reality-free writeup, completely detached from earthly considerations, is when a writer talks about "Blockchain", capital B, no "the".* You should try mentally replacing the word

---

\*   I commend to you "Ignoring Blockchain Is Corporate Suicide: Why Blockchain is the biggest single threat to all CEOs for destroying corporate value" by Nick Ayton, in analyst newsletter *Innovation Enterprise* (7 July 2016). In the several years I've been following Bitcoin and blockchains, this is the single worst and most incoherent piece of "Blockchain" hype I've seen; you definitely need to read it,

"Blockchain" with "Cloud" and see if the article seems eerily familiar. Also try the previous business technology buzzwords "big data", "NoSQL", "SaaS" and "Web 2.0," and see how it works with those.

## But all these companies are using Blockchain now!

They almost certainly aren't.

Blockchain marketers consistently claim some prominent company "is using" a blockchain when there's just been a press release that they're running a vendor trial, or "investigating" running a future trial. This is because an "investigation" is cheap – this book is a legitimate business expense for this purpose, by the way – and worth the PR value in showing you're fully up to date with current buzzwords. "Researching the opportunities" *could* mean anything, but almost certainly *does* mean nothing.

The Bitcoin press is composed of advocacy blogs enthusiastically promoting anything to do with cryptos, because what their readership wants is reassurance that this is the future (and that their Bitcoin holding will go to the moon). Even when covering actual news, the journalism tends to be ridiculously sloppy. (In using these as sources

---

to inoculate yourself against the worst excesses of this foolishness.

Ayton spends the first third of the article repeating how devastating Blockchain will be to business, the second third making technically garbled or meaningless unsubstantiated claims about the future and the last third on a list of predictions, many of which have already been shown unfeasible and three or four of which are literally out of '80s cyberpunk science fiction, as if he read too much William Gibson as a lad and thinks Blockchain will make *Mona Lisa Overdrive* real – "augmented reality using VR and holographic systems will feed off sensory layers that will sit on the Ledger of Things connecting the world", presumably visible to your new Zeiss-Ikon eyeballs.

"Someone asked me what Ethereum was… My response: 'Imagine giving the Internet a dose of Viagra and increasing the dose each day'… The Blockchain Age is here!"

I know of one case where a non-technical manager inadvertently sent this link around their company; they quickly realised how relentlessly terrible everything about blockchains actually is – anyone who's survived in business where sales people exist doesn't need to be a techie to notice there's something deeply wrong and lacking in blockchain hype – but the article had by then caught the attention of upper management. The manager found themselves in the position of designated expert and having to quell this idea, mostly by a process of translating why none of this could ever work into sober and considered business speak from the original profanity-laced screaming.

for this book, I've had to carefully double-check any given claim isn't aspirational rubbish, and I've probably missed a few.) They write articles about things that have not happened yet and probably won't. "Talking about" becomes "considering doing," becomes "will do," becomes "is doing." Even if a given blockchain trial does in fact happen, later failure is not documented.

The mainstream press assume this is specialist press rather than boosterism, and run stories taking all this at face value. As the buzzword "Blockchain" has gained currency, they have tended to run blockchain marketers' press releases barely edited, assuming there must be something to all of this. (IBM have put out a lot of these lately.)

As one otherwise very blockchain-positive paper, TechUK's "Industrialisation of Distributed Ledger Technology in Banking and Financial Services," puts it:[334]

> There is currently no commercially available proven technology platform tested for enterprise class volume, security, reliability and regulations yet. This is one of the key factors holding back the productive implementation of the use cases. To date for conducting POCs,[*] banks have used available open source or vendor technologies. Several compromises or assumptions can be made at POC stage but these cannot be carried on to production systems.

If you see a use case that catches your attention, a web search on the company names and the word "blockchain" will often track down the original press release. Check very carefully which details are clearly substantiated in the present tense, and which are aspirational.

## Blockchains won't clean up your data for you

When blockchain schemes do promise some specific outcome, it's usually the magic of full availability of properly cleaned up and standardised data. The actual problem is cleaning up the data in the first place, or getting legacy systems talking to each other at all.

In finance in particular, the back-office systems are decades old and won't interoperate without tremendous effort. For all the considerable effort at computerisation, there's still too much paper

---

[*]    Proofs of concept.

and human effort. Settlements can still take days. Wall Street was *very* receptive to the blockchain pitch.[335]

The blockchain proponents' business goal is to become the organisation controlling the new data standard, with a monopoly maintained by network effect. The barrier that such efforts founder on, over and over – and did before anyone tried adding blockchains to the idea – is that no industry's players want to create a new central octopus.

Examples include:

- Blem Information Management, an insurance software company, posit putting all documents on a blockchain so smart contracts can speed up payouts. The problem this claims to solve is insurers deliberately altering or losing documents: "There have always been suspicions that insurers could change the data on what the situation was in the past."[336] It's not explained how an insurer prepared to commit blatant fraud could be trusted to pay a claim anyway.

    Assessing claims is in fact the hard part, and claims adjustment is done by humans talking to humans. The proposal uses smart contracts to speed up processing claims – which just moves all the back-office computing from the insurer to the miners of the blockchain in question.

- Land title registers on a blockchain solves no part of the actual problem with land title registry: parcels of land that have an owner but have escaped being put on the existing official register.[337] Storing the official register on a blockchain offers no advantage over having it in an ordinary database (which you can already distribute authenticated copies of), and no digital record will enforce land use for you.

- Supply chain provenance is a perennial proposal. Provenance, Inc. proposes putting tuna catches on the Ethereum blockchain. They claim to offer supply chain transparency to all participants, and this will reveal illegal overfishing or fishing that involves human rights abuses.

    The data would still be entered by local humans under the auspices of "trusted" local NGOs who pay monthly for the software. The assumption seems to be that commercial operations engaging in illegal overfishing or human rights abuses will carefully document their illegal activities on the blockchain and not just *lie*, or bribe the "neutral" inspectors or adjudicators – as happens in current supply chain monitoring.[338]

The main byproduct is a monopoly for the traceability provider, *i.e.*, Provenance. Their own white paper simultaneously claims the system is "decentralized" but with a centrally-controlled "Provenance-validated chain of custody."[339] The actual present-day problem turns out to be no agreement on what data to collect or what to do with it.

- Almost every proposed music industry case (see next chapter).

These also have a galloping case of the "oracle problem": getting good real-world data into the blockchain in the first place requires human judgement.

(Some blockchain hype talks about "artificial intelligence on the blockchain." If someone tries this one, drill down for details of their artificial intelligence product.)

If your big goal is cleaned-up and standardised data across multiple organisations, the only approach likely to get you there is creating a data schema that is so obviously and elegantly the right thing that everyone just adopts it themselves as the *de facto* standard, and a standards body or regulator eventually says "hey, use this one." Note lack of blockchains. (This is the usual approach in computing, though even there companies routinely try to set themselves up in the role of central octopus.) And obviously, the blockchain won't replace your back-office systems without as much work, time and money as any other software replacement project would be.

Getting funding at long last to clean up your data and formats may be worth saying the word "blockchain." Matt Levine from *Bloomberg* notes: "The word 'blockchain' has managed to make that boring back-office coordination work sexy, which means that it might actually get done."[340] This, rather than anything blockchains themselves offer, seems to be the most productive result of business blockchain trials to date. Once that's in place, you can increase efficiency markedly by taking the blockchain bit out.

## Six questions to ask your blockchain salesman

If someone is trying to sell you on blockchains, the obvious skeptical questions will get you a long way:

- Are they confusing "might" and "is"? (*Almost all* business blockchain claims are full of "might" and salespeople talking about "the possibilities.") Do they have present-day working blockchains that do every one of the things they've claimed you can get from blockchains? If not, which ones are missing?

- Will the system scale to the size of your data? How?

- How do you deal with human error in the "immutable" blockchain or smart contracts?

- If this is for working with people you trust less than the people you deal with now, how are they assuring the security of the chain – what's the security threat model? (Get your system administrator along to ask pointed questions.)

- If it's for working with people you can already trust to that degree, why are you bothering with a blockchain?

- What does this get you that a centralised database can't? How, precisely? (Drill down.)

## Security threat models

If you want to work with people you trust less than those you trust now, you will need to be absolutely clear on how your blockchain is secured against attackers, both internal and external.

What is your threat model? What attacks from the outside world do you need to protect against? What attacks from your fellows on your blockchain do you need to protect against? What do your security-conscious IT staff think of all this?

Attacks may include:[341]

- The usual human problems in cryptographic key management. Ordinary employees just trying to do their jobs are *really bad* at security thinking. What can someone do as "you" if your company's keys leak, or if someone clicks the wrong link in a phishing email?

- If you have enough hashpower on a Proof of Work chain, from 25% up you can conduct an attack on the system, as described in the Bitcoin mining chapter. In Bitcoin, this attacks the transaction ledger; in a business blockchain, the integrity of the information.

- On an invitation-only permissioned blockchain, you don't have to control a large chunk of the hash power – you just need to compromise a single member.

- The miner gets to choose which transactions they write to the next block. What could they write, or decline to write, to the chain that would be adverse to you? What if some other members of your chain decide they don't like you?

Blockchain promises that it will let people who don't trust each other work together. The trouble is that it does this only approximately, with startling inefficiency, and in a way that naturally recentralises to one or a few winners, as happened with Bitcoin. The usual proposal to avoid this is to just start with central authority, at which point you probably shouldn't be using a blockchain.

# Permissioned blockchains

Exposing all your business data and back-office machinery to the whole Internet is obviously silly. So the next move was *permissioned blockchains*, for approved users only.

There are various *consensus models*, or ways to choose who gets to write the next block. Bitcoin-style competitive Proof of Work is stupendously wasteful. Most permissioned blockchains use something else, typically various forms of just agreeing to take turns, because trustlessness in practice is hugely inefficient, and a bit of trust saves vast amounts of wasted effort.

But even then, a "permissioned" blockchain is otherwise known as "the most inefficient possible centrally-administered database cluster." All proposals I've seen in the course of researching this chapter, if they turned out to do anything useful, could gain *immediate* performance improvements by just moving to a conventional centralised database.

You already work with other people and companies. Industry consortia, standards groups and so on are well-tested models. Blockchains do not offer a better way to do this.

An August 2015 blog post from Vitalik Buterin discusses "public", "consortium" and "private" blockchains. Bitcoin and Ethereum are "public" blockchains.[342] This comment chain on the post concisely summarises the innovations the private blockchain brings:

*Andrey Zamovskiy:* Let's just admit that blockchain is simply a new type of replication algorithm for a database cluster. That's it.

*Vitalik Buterin:* Correct. Plus Merkle trees. The Merkle trees are actually important.

*Andrey Zamovskiy:* Merkle trees have not been invented with bitcoin, they've just got an adoption.

Of course, one use case is that a "private blockchain"[343] or "mutualized database structure"[344] might sound less suspect to anti-trust authorities than a "cartel". And the desire to get out from under the gimlet eye of regulators post-2008 attracts the more adventurous sort of financial firm looking for a suitable "dark pool" of liquidity.[345] The next economic disaster courtesy irresponsible speculation is hardly going to cause itself, after all.

In practice, financial institutions talking up "Blockchain" are envisaging a private permissioned blockchain, with only well-known participants, and only as open as regulators require.

## Beneficiaries of business Blockchain

The market for selling buzzwords to upper management has done very well with "Blockchain," which is vastly superior to "cloud computing" or "NoSQL" in not being verifiably any particular sort of product whatsoever. Which means it can be *any* product, at least hypothetically.

People selling buzzwords to venture capitalists have benefited similarly. There's been about $1.5 billion in venture capital spent on Bitcoin-related ventures up to February 2017, which have so far returned zero;[346] the word "Bitcoin" is now a red flag to venture capitalists, so a quick terminology shift is most useful.

Any business that involves records or logs of any sort can quickly add the word "blockchain" to improve its marketability and further the all-important press release churnalism and "Ten Hot Startups" listings to back its flimsy promotional Wikipedia entry.

Even if your product has nothing to do with blockchains, you can talk about blockchains to suggest people use your thing instead while they're waiting for blockchains that work.[347]

# Non-beneficiaries of business Blockchain

A keen prospective market is end users who want efficiency savings and will even look into magical flying unicorn ponies to see if they can get them. None of these have found any in blockchains.

The most prominent current attempt is the Australian Securities Exchange (ASX) testing a blockchain-based replacement for its 24-year-old back-office settlement software; they're working with Digital Asset Holdings, so this might actually involve a blockchain proper. Many of the claims are pure hype, *e.g.*, they appear to have been sold the pup "instant transaction clearance,"[348] and their customers are already deeply unhappy that the ASX are not proposing something that talks a more industry standard protocol.

"We think if we can get this right, we can get very close to real-time settlement. You should be able to sell shares at your desk right now and walk to the nearest ATM to get your money. That is our mission," said then-CEO Elmer Funke Kupper. Such short block times are unlikely to be sufficiently secure for a system with serious money in it, far outweighing the comparatively piddling amounts in Bitcoin or the DAO, and with a concomitant level of hostile attacker; it is possible that Digital Asset Holdings did not outline this problem to him.

Funke Kupper resigned in August 2016 after a bribery allegation; the new CEO has said he's staying the course,[349] but has also punted the decision into the long grass.[350]

Real businesses don't in fact want the world seeing all their transactions, which is where the idea of private blockchains comes from. As IBM found out *after* starting Hyperledger, all manner of businesses – financial institutions, beef industry, shoe brands, confectioners – don't want to share data even with all participants in their blockchain, but only with the people the specific deal is actually with.[351 352 353] This was apparently news to them. It turns out that IBM set up an elaborate hammer design consortium without first finding out if there are nails.

## "Blockchain" products you can buy!

With so many people waving money and shouting "SELL ME A BLOCKCHAIN! WHATEVER THAT IS," several companies have come forth to offer something using that word and fulfilling at least a few of the less outlandish claims.

This is easier than you might think, since the actually good bit is the tamper-evident ledger, and we already have working examples which are useful for real things (*e.g.*, Git) with no need for the sillier aspects of blockchain-style decentralisation.

The examples remain instructive, particularly in comparison to Bitcoin or Ethereum:

**Accenture:** Accenture offer the one thing customers who actually have money want from a blockchain: centralised administration and a way to edit the ledger when necessary. You might think that this is literally the opposite of the standard blockchain value proposition since the invention of Bitcoin, but Accenture probably have a better track record of big-ticket sales. They mention The DAO as an excellent worked example of why this is needed.[354]

**Microsoft:** Azure Blockchain as a Service promises public, consortium or private blockchains, with any consensus algorithm you like, definitely reaching public release status with at least some of the promised features some time soon maybe. You will be able to write smart contracts in Solidity, offering all the advantages of that language that we've already seen with The DAO.[355]

**Hyperledger:** IBM offer the IBM Blockchain, based on Hyperledger. Hyperledger.org is a corporate open source Potemkin village of the sort IBM has long favoured: the illusion of an open project, with no "there" there. I spent half an hour dredging the site and could not find one clear statement of *what this software is actually intended to do*, let alone differences from and similarities to existing blockchains. Even Bitcoin blog *CoinDesk* notes: "Among the doubts facing Hyperledger is a perceived lack of clarity on what might be ultimately produced by the initiative."[356]

If you click long enough, you'll find a page where the participating companies have dumped their unfinished blockchain experiments.[357] The main code contributor is Digital Asset Holdings; their joining announcement (on their own site, not hyperledger.org) gives as technical details only that Hyperledger is an append-only ledger and has an actual Bitcoin-style blockchain in it.[358] (Digital Asset Holdings was founded by Blythe Masters, pioneer of the credit default swap, the financial instrument behind the global financial crisis of 2008 that may have provoked Nakamoto to finally release Bitcoin.)

**Sawtooth Lake:** Intel's contribution to Hyperledger.org replaces the blitheringly stupid and wasteful Proof of Work with something equally stupid but less wasteful, Proof of Elapsed Time,[359] which might as well be called Proof of Buying An Intel CPU. Rather than have miners compete to produce the next block, a timer running in an environment secured by a DRM mechanism built into your Intel CPU picks if you get to do the next block. The white paper is an extended advertisement for Intel® Software Guard Extensions™ (SGX™). Also, they only have a *simulated* Proof of Buying An Intel CPU mechanism as yet.

This doesn't provide any security against malicious participants, on the logic that private blockchains need speed over security. You might think that at that point you don't need a blockchain at all, but you're hardly going to sell any consultant hours with *that* sort of thinking.

**Chain Core:** Software to run a permissioned private "blockchain". It solves the secure distributed consensus problem in an obvious and sensible manner: blocks are generated only by designated official core nodes.[360] Distributed consensus is so much simpler if you don't distribute it. 2016 press stories that Visa was using it in the real world were in fact *forward-looking* versions of Visa's press release that they were planning a pilot programme for 2017.[361]

**R3 Corda:** The R3 Consortium's Corda Distributed Ledger Designed for Financial Services is the most sensible of all these approaches: after careful consideration of the fact that the Bitcoin-style blockchain was expressly designed to be the direct opposite of what large paying customers with money want, their "Blockchain Product" does not, in its default configuration … contain a blockchain.[362]

# UK Government Office for Science: "Distributed Ledger Technology: beyond block chain"

The UK's Chief Scientific Adviser, Sir Mark Walpole, released a report in January 2016, "Distributed Ledger Technology: beyond block chain,"[363] which caught some attention at the time, as an official government publication concerning the issue.

The report's existence suggests high-level interest, but it is not a good report and won't inform you in any manner – it was literally written by the companies and consultants selling blockchain and smart contract hype, the overview buys the hype wholesale with fantastic claims of present-day capabilities that are not true of any existing blockchain, its "case studies" are largely hypothetical and it has way too many typos for a report anyone cared about at any stage. It reads like an end-of-term assignment written in a single desperate overnight caffeinated tour de force. The accompanying video[364] is vastly improved if you imagine it being narrated by Philomena Cunk.

The meat of the report is a complicated plan to put all UK welfare spending on a single blockchain, purchases only being possible through a DRMed smartphone, for the purpose of fine-grained monitoring of spending habits. The noteworthy thing about this plan is how there is nothing feasible about any aspect of it.

The report's recommendations are largely generic, the important one being that the government should run local trials involving blockchains. None of these have shown up in the ensuing months, but there may be opportunities for sale and ongoing maintenance contracts on technology that can't possibly ever work properly.

# Chapter 12: Case study: Why you can't put the music industry on a blockchain

The recording industry has suffered nearly two decades of crisis, after the 1990s CD boom petered out and the Internet proceeded to turn the entire world of human communication upside down. The musicians themselves are no happier. In an instructive worked example of Blockchain hype in one industry, both sides have heard the word "blockchain" and wonder if it could be their saviour.

Jeremy Silver of Digital Catapult quotes Mark Meharry, CEO of MusicGlue, as calling "blockchain" the "worst case of smoke and mirrors" that he has seen in an industry which "specialises in self-deception". Nevertheless, the wants and needs behind music industry blockchain dreams are worth exploring.

## The rights management quagmire

Any piece of music has many intertwined rights. There's the copyright in the music and the words, the copyright in a given recording of the song, the right to reproduce a recording mechanically, the right to public performance, the right to broadcast, the use of a recording in a film or video, whatever rights are involved in streaming – still a subject of much negotiation – different laws in different countries ... and these get even more complicated when there are samples of previous works involved.

Keeping track of all of this is a huge amount of labour-intensive back office faff. The systems are creaky, haphazard and ill-maintained. All the incentives are *not* to fix it, because that would mean more efficient payouts.

The back office can be horrifyingly slapdash. Real example: one US rights management operation specialising in an obscure subgenre which turns out to be used in a lot of movies. Their accountants had to first keep running, then later emulating, 32-bit operating systems because the company's custom software was written in the DOS era.

The majority of payments in the subgenre were stalled for three weeks in 2014 as the accountants waited on a back-ordered 32-bit Windows 7 PC, because a software rewrite (or even just running it in DOSbox) was vetoed by the company's owner. Now multiply this by an industry.

Even ASCAP, a membership-based nonprofit collection society, for a long time consigned the job of paying people properly to the "too hard" basket – they would collect performance fees from *all* venues, but would only pay performance royalties to the top 200 grossing tours that year; indie musicians were literally subsidising the biggest rock stars.[365] This only changed after widespread negative publicity.[366]

If the money funnel gets at all complicated, the agencies often just give up and hand the artist's money to a large company. Real example: a US-based songwriter is a member of ASCAP. Their song sells a download in Japan. The shop pays the local agency, JASRAC, for public performance. JASRAC splits the money as 30% public performance and 70% mechanical royalties – an arbitrary split varying per country. JASRAC takes 15-25% for administration and passes the rest of the 30% public performance to ASCAP. If you or your label don't reach out and claim the 70% mechanical, it's split per total market share between the major record labels locally. Each step of the process involves months of delays and is almost impossible to audit.

This can become a point of competition. Music services company Kobalt, for example, have cut a swathe through the industry in the past few years with a data-driven approach that pays musicians relatively fast.[367] (And has no use for blockchains.) SoundExchange works similarly.

## Getting paid for your song

The artist, of course, gets paid only after everyone else's cut, if at all.

Then there's whether as an artist your deals concerning these rights are even fair. And the bit where you try to extract the money that is owed to you from large companies, and their offices around the world.

There are various agencies that offer to handle all of this for you, because there's never been a shortage of helpful people keen to intermediate between you, the *artist*, and the prospect of money. So along come companies promising to do this on a "blockchain" using "smart contracts" that can't be weaseled out of and will pay you in less than a year. It sounds almost too good to be true!

## The record industry's loss of control and the streaming apocalypse

The record companies' fundamental problem is that they no longer control studio access, pressing plant access or distribution – you can record on a laptop and sell your music online, or just give it away. Anyone on the whole Internet can be an artist, and you're in direct competition with all of them. And the marginal cost of a copy is zero, and your customers know it.

There's a lot of bitterness and resentment – the record industry blames Apple and Google for the fact of technology, even though all of this could have been reasonably anticipated in the late 1980s from the existence of the early Internet and psychoacoustic lossy compression (the basis of MP3). Their response to every new technology since the cassette has been to try to strangle it in the crib. Their consistent strategy concerning the Internet, the greatest revolution in human communication since the printing press, has been to try to hobble it.

They tried to stop piracy with Digital Rights Management (DRM), which bred massive consumer resentment and meant that piracy literally gave listeners a better product than the paid version. This peaked with the Sony rootkit malware fiasco of 2005, where if you put a CD into your PC, it would install a hidden software backdoor that blocked CD ripping, phoned home to Sony and left new security holes for other malware to use.[368] And DRM can't possibly work in the first place – you can't give someone the lock and the key, then keep the key secret from them forever. No DRM that end users wanted to break has ever stayed unbroken.

The income levels of the 1990s CD boom turned out not to be a law of nature, and streaming has seen people move their music listening from CDs to something very like radio – much as when radio sent US record sales from 100 million in 1930 to 6 million in 1932.

(And there was a depression then, too. The music industry lives *entirely* off people's discretionary income, which is highly sensitive to consumer confidence. When times are tough, attitudes are hard.)

The record business has no idea how to deal with the Internet, and there seems no obvious solution. This is like catnip for snake-oil salesmen: desperate people with money to spend. Perhaps "blockchains" will fix it!

## Berklee Rethink and blockchain dreams

The blockchain hype went public in July 2015 with "Fair Music: Transparency and Payment Flows in the Music Industry,"[369] a report from the Rethink Music initiative at the Berklee College of Music's Institute for Creative Entrepreneurship.

The problems it outlines are well-known and widely acknowledged:

- Who owns what is frequently not traceable at all. "20-50 percent of music payments don't make it to their rightful owners." Music collection societies tried to create a Global Repertoire Database in the early 2010s, but scrapped the idea in 2014, as nobody wanted to create a new central octopus.[370].

- Existing industry money flows are an unbelievably complicated mess that's barely understood by most participants.

- Middlemen take money without any reasonable present-day justification.

- Record and publishing companies deliberately obscure what they owe and who they owe it to,[371] and pay *very* slowly.

- Streaming doesn't pay nearly as well as CDs used to. (That last problem is not like the others, but keeps being spoken of like it is.)

The report proposes: (a) gather data about as many of these deals as possible, to make the problems clear, (b) revise the contractual arrangements of literally the entire recording industry worldwide, and – in half a page tacked on the end – (c) keep the entire details of every deal the recording industry has ever done and continues to do on a blockchain and (d) administer the deals using smart contracts.

Specifically, it suggests:

- Rights ownership and royalty splits that are recorded on the blockchain, money being automatically redirected accordingly, *e.g.,* directly upon an iTunes purchase;
- Transactions that occur "nearly instantaneously" ("in less than one second") and directly, from consumer to artist without intermediaries.

Of course, the word "blockchain" caught all press attention, and not any of the real problems the rest of the paper described.

# Imogen Heap: "Tiny Human". Total sales: $133.20.

Others had already been thinking along blockchain lines. Imogen Heap has been recording through major labels for a couple of decades now, first with the duo Frou Frou and then as a solo singer, songwriter and producer. In the course of a string of chart hits and Grammy nominations, she's suffered quite her share of duplicitous incompetence at the hands of the music industry, and wants something better.

In late 2015, Heap found herself free of previous deals, and so released her new song "Tiny Human" as the test case for Mycelia,[*] running on the Ethereum blockchain. Her motivation was to cut through the tangle of bad deals and obscure rights the record industry offered. "Its success will come from the adoption of millions of music lovers."[372] Mycelia worked with Ujo Music, an attempt to automate the back-room disbursement side put together by Ethereum development company ConsenSys, whose Vinay Gupta had first told Heap about smart contracts.

Heap's explicit goal is to have all music you've "bought" (not just hers) behave as marketing spyware that collects data on the user, in the manner of advertising trackers on web pages:[†]

---

[*]   There's a famous saying concerning mushrooms and distributing information.

[†]   Imogen Heap. "What Blockchain Can Do for the Music Industry". *Demos Quarterly* #8, Spring 2016. I've also had reports of discussions with the people behind the "Tiny Human" initiative, and a musical ecosystem with the functionality I describe as "spyware" is absolutely the intention. (Also, they dislike Bandcamp.)

We know less about what our songs get up to once they've left 'home'. What would I like to read on these postcards from our songs? Well, how many times it was played, by who and where would be a great start.

The last Imogen Heap release with spyware was the 2005 *Speak For Yourself* CD with Sony's rootkit malware – an initiative that didn't go down so well then either.

The press coverage of Heap's new initiative was vast, and her name is still routinely brought up whenever blockchaining the music industry is mentioned. What I've yet to see anyone mention is how well it did in practice. Total sales of "Tiny Human" through Ujo Music on the Ethereum blockchain were ... $133.20. Not $133,200 – but one hundred and thirty-three dollars and twenty cents: 222 sales at 60 cents each. It literally got more press articles than sales. It was taken off sale some time in 2016.

It didn't help that buying it was almost impossible even for a blockchain advocate,[373] let alone an ordinary human music fan. You went to the page, clicked "Download", followed the instructions to create an Ethereum wallet, and went off to a Bitcoin exchange to buy bitcoins then exchange those for ether, as ETH wasn't widely traded directly to dollars at the time. Getting hold of the bitcoins required you either to send your money and a pile of government identification to an unregulated exchange – the recommended exchange, ShapeShift, had literally left New York state to avoid anti-money-laundering regulations[374] – deal with crooks or both. Once you'd done all this, you got a download key. The process was ridiculously glitchy and buggy. "The exact ether amount is a bit of a gamble."[375]

Ujo Music later posted a rambling nonexcuse for the "Tiny Human" disaster, in which they admitted that they'd only researched what the hell they were doing after they'd done it. "We are but a few bright-eyed technologists with a special hammer, looking for the right nail."[376]

You'd think that at that point Heap would be wishing she'd just put it up on Bandcamp, but she's still pursuing the blockchain dream and selling others on it, particularly the Featured Artists Coalition, *i.e.,* the stars who did quite well out of the old major label system and would like to keep something that works like that did. Never give up!

A record shop *must not* be harder to use than BitTorrent. The legal options, iTunes, Netflix and Spotify, made it big by being *more convenient than piracy*, and there is *nothing* convenient about dealing with blockchains. For buying music online, Bandcamp has all comers beat for a record shop experience that delights both buyers and sellers,[377] pays 85% to the artist and doesn't have any use for a blockchain.

# Why blockchains are a bad fit for music

It's immediately obvious that blockchains proper – even if euphemised to Distributed Ledger Technology – can't possibly be the panacea the record industry desperately desires.

No single blockchain can possibly scale to the whole music industry. There were an estimated 35 million songs in iTunes in 2013[378]; Spotify played *a billion* streams a day by mid-2015.[379] If you use multiple blockchains, they will need reconciliation.

Apart from the metadata itself being *huge*, there's the encoded details of all the hundred-page contracts. Who are the participants in the blockchain who will each be keeping their own copy of all of this data? And who will pay for the computing resources to execute all the smart contracts for each song played?

(Posited solutions include storing contract details off-chain on the BitTorrent-like InterPlanetary File System, so you'd better hope there's still a node that can seed a full copy of your publishing deal thirty years later! Also, the IPFS doesn't work yet.)

"Where there's a hit, there's a writ." Data will change – erroneous or fraudulent claims, copyright lawsuits changing ownership information, you litigate your way free of your awful first contract, a musician dies. How is your "immutable" blockchain corrected?

What's your security threat model? This one never seems to be mentioned, and we're talking about real-world money here. How is your blockchain kept secure against hostile attackers, *e.g.*, someone who has the money to bring 51% of mining resources to bear against a Proof of Work secured chain? How will you clean up the mess after an attacker uses bugs in your smart contract platform that they knew existed and you didn't?

# Attempts to make sense of the hype

As blockchain proposals proliferate, so do industry white papers frantically trying to make sense of all of this.

The basic claims advanced by Blockchain for Creative Industries' extensively publicised "Music On The Blockchain"[380] (foreword by Nick Mason of Pink Floyd) are highly questionable:

> BCI regard the prospect of a networked database of music copyright information, near-instant micropayments, transparency through the value chain and access to alternative sources of capital as the four key potential benefits of blockchain technology for the record industry, though even these are not without their challenges.

That's an understatement. (They also think Proof of Work is a great idea and not a naturally-centralising ecological disaster.) BCI acknowledge as problems:

- A cryptographic hash won't prevent copying.

- Who enters the data? How is the data verified? (The oracle problem.)

- Credit and splits are often negotiated well after the writing or recording.

- Promises of a "fair trade music ecosystem" founder on the obvious problem that "it is not clear that all parties understand fairness or fair trade in the same way."

- Which blockchain does all this run on, what cryptocurrency is our medium of exchange? Are any technically up to the task? (*spoiler:* no.)

MusicTechFest's "#MTFLabs: Blockchain" meeting[381] broke down on the problem that the various players have *always* had contradictory interests, viciously fought, and moving the perpetual industry civil war to the blockchain probably won't help much:

> In large part due to the inherent fault lines within the topic itself, the lab turned away from seeking "solutions" to discussing concepts such as "copyright", "ownership" and "security", as such words can take on very different meanings based on one's professional background and personal frames. Differences in perception revealed seemingly intractable

disagreements that were unlikely to be resolved in a weeklong discussion about an incredibly complex technology.

> … As tensions grew over fundamental differences in perception and the complexity of the issue expanded the more its core limitations were revealed, the effort to arrive at even the most basic conclusions nearly collapsed.

Their paper notes the things the blockchain can't do for you:

- DRM, which still can't work.
- Storing large amounts of data, *e.g.*, song files.
- Doing all this for free. You'll need some way to pay for all the computing resources this will need, and there will probably need to be fees for all of the hypothesised transactions.

They propose:

> a modular approach, where specific problems are solved incrementally, building up an open and transparent meta-system ensuring the individual systems that address the sub-problems use open standards and globally acceptable and accessible data, for example residing in one or more blockchain-based systems.

This is likely the only workable approach to the global metadata problem – come up with a usable open standard that's sufficiently self-evidently correct that others adopt it – except there's no reason to use a blockchain for this.

"Blockchain or the Chaingang?" by Jeremy Silver[382] is the best and clearest survey I've found of blockchain dreams and how they relate to music industry psychology. It's not perfect on technical detail, but you don't need to be a techie to know what snake-oil salesmen sound like.

Silver outlines many of the obvious problems with musical blockchains:

- The really obvious scaling problems.
- Music industry blockchain maximalists are sincere but misguided, and want technically infeasible things.
- Blockchain dreams require DRM: "adding the transactional security is key to what blockchain does. That has to be one of its key selling points."

- Heap's idea of full metadata on everything about a song, and deals not being secret, is fundamentally good. (Even if listening to a record being turned into an opportunity for spyware has a few issues.) But blockchains won't somehow clean up the metadata that the Global Repertoire Database hoped to gather, and that data's still hugely in flux (when there's a hit, there's a writ).

- As in every other industry that's tried reconciling all the data, Global Repertoire Database-type proposals fail when everyone realises they're about to give the metadata maintainer a natural monopoly.

- Incumbents will treat technological change as a threat and resist it as bitterly as they have every other technology. Silver notes major labels *refusing* to look at BitTorrent data his firm Semetric was offering them, even though it was an excellent predictor of sales, for fear of appearing to validate BitTorrent in any manner.

The one point I think Silver slips on is near the conclusion:

> From a purely pragmatic perspective, if you asked a technologist today what would be the most efficient system to build, using current technologies, to create a royalties tracking, gathering and distribution system, they would probably tell you it was blockchain.

*Let me just differ on that one.* That said, Silver is confident enough in his conclusion that he's now CEO of Digital Catapult, a consultancy who enthusiastically offer business blockchain services, even if some of their promotional material is disconcertingly aspirational.[383]

## Other musical blockchain initiatives

All of these have as their business plan to become the new central octopus, or at least one of several.

In the wake of its report, **Berklee** has started its own Open Music Initiative, to do what the Global Repertoire Database tried to, with blockchains thrown in to no obvious utility.[384]

**PeerTracks** is one of several companies attempting to set up a system where every artist would sell their own separate cryptocurrency tokens as shares in their future earnings, and streaming royalties would be allocated to the owners of the tokens via smart contracts.[385] Apparently the buyers would be the artist's fans rather than music industry companies. Founder Cédric Cobban subscribes to Austrian economics, which led him to Bitcoin and then this idea.[386]

Benji Rogers of the **dot.blockchain** initiative pushes a holistic vision to which the entire industry would need to subscribe, revolving around his ".bc" file format, which he swears up and down is *not at all* Digital Rights Management, which customers despise – it's Digital Rights *Expression*, which plays only on compliant platforms that only let you do permitted things with it and formats that don't do this shouldn't be allowed to exist.[387] This is literally the approach that crashed and burned hard enough in the early 2000s to make "DRM" a curse to this day. Also, everything should involve Virtual Reality, for some reason. And the InterPlanetary File System, which if it worked would still be a new form of BitTorrent.

**Revelator** promises a generic buzzword soup of rights management, instant transactions, micropayments and "disruptive technologies", to demonstrate the actual point of much of this: getting funding from venture capitalists. You'll be pleased to know they say it's all about the *art*.[388]

**The TAO** is a smart contracts-based rights administrator selling ~~unregistered securities~~ shares to raise development funds. They explicitly invoke The DAO as their model, which is a *bold* tack to take after July 2016.[389]

All these competing systems speak of *the artist* as their only and eternal concern. But the TAO promoted its share offering with news of a label putting all their artists on the TAO just like that, suggesting that artists in the new world will play a role much like their present one, *i.e.*, a sort of industrially-processed cheese slice.

Are you supposed to sign up with some of these systems? All of them? Why? How are disputes with your blockchain-based rights management organisation handled? Perhaps your contract with them could go on a blockchain.

(So sorry, our smart contract got hacked! All your money is gone. Yes, yours in particular. No, we can't get it back, smart contract says no. Well, you *could* sue, I suppose. How much money have you got? Oh, none? What a pity. Never mind.)

# SingularDTV

The SingularDTV initiative is sufficiently remarkable to cover in depth. SingularDTV takes this tottering heap of bad ideas and uses it to implement another tottering heap of bad ideas.

SingularDTV is a platform for filmmakers and TV producers to fund their content and then distribute it. This involves a native ICO-style cryptocurrency token called SNGLS (running on the Ethereum blockchain), with funding and revenues administered by a smart contract called CODE.[390]

This is the poison pill: it runs on their token, and they control the software that reads it. If they get greedy — and really, when has anyone with power in the entertainment industry ever gotten greedy? — your "immutable" and "decentralised" ledger may turn out to be neither, as happened with The DAO. There will be heartfelt excuses.

SNGLS were sold in an ICO and are traded on the cryptocurrency exchanges. The offer document for their unregistered security[391] went out the door a bit early:

> User has carefully reviewed the code of the Smart Contract System located on the Ethereum blockchain at the addresses set forth under [correct cite] and fully understands and accepts the functions implemented therein;

The closest they have to a technologist on the SingularDTV executive is Joseph Lubin of the Ethereum Foundation and ConsenSys, the company developing their smart contract. Everyone else appears to be a media industry person, which leaves SingularDTV looking very like the standard marketing of DRM snake oil to desperate old media.

SingularDTV's stated goal in their white paper[392] is *two million* paid viewings per episode, at $2.60 a go — in ether, not actual dollars — of a planned TV show over the next two to three years. They give no basis for this number, nor where millions of new Ethereum users will come from, nor why millions of ordinary suburban consumers won't find hitting the Pirate Bay vastly more convenient than dealing in ether and having "sorry for your loss" events. (Though they have a seven-minute SingularDTV Lightwallet Instructional Video.) Perhaps they can gross even more than $133.20.

Why would someone think such a ridiculously flimsy scheme was a good and workable idea? Their totally boss sci-fi TV series

*Singularity*, no less! A worldwide economic collapse, as predicted by Austrian economics, leads to a fictional Caribbean island becoming the richest place in the world because it was first to adopt Ethereum as its currency. Then an artificial intelligence takes over the world, rendering the preceding plot meaningless. To be produced and distributed worldwide through the S-DTV portal!

They are so keen on their sci-fi TV show idea that they named their blockchain startup after it. It appears that they are in fact Singularitarians — fans of Ray Kurzweil's non-musical-instrument ideas, like an artificial intelligence taking over the world this century — who came up with a way to propagandise their beliefs in Ethereum and the Singularity (and crank pseudoeconomics) through the medium of science fiction television, and decided a crypto asset offering was clearly the way to collect money to make the TV show to evangelise their cult.[393]

## Summary

Blockchains won't solve your bad recording or publishing deal. They can't scale to collecting your money from the main channels, let alone other countries or obscure sources. They won't extract money from Spotify or YouTube they don't have – Spotify's haemorrhaging red ink as it is.[394] Just assume the major labels will hand the whole industry over to Apple a *second* time.

If you want to clean up industry metadata, blockchains aren't going to do that for you. What will is some way to clean it up that doesn't involve creating a new organisation you can't trust. Something along the lines of MTFLabs' incremental approach is probably the only one with a chance.

# Conclusion

I started this book in October 2016 and finished the first draft in December. Had I tried to say then what was coming next in cryptos, there is no way I would have foreseen the six months since.

I would have predicted that Bitcoin would continue to be clogged and barely usable for real purchases, licit or illicit. I'd have thought Ethereum would keep stumbling along, with no real application being found for smart contracts. I'd have forecast "Blockchain" slowly falling out of favour as a business buzzword as the returns failed to manifest.

I would not have predicted a second bubble in Bitcoin, with tabloid newspaper finance sections enthusing about the fabulous potential of cryptocurrencies to normal people who have no business going within a mile of such horrifyingly risky investments. I would not have anticipated a matching bubble in Ethereum, and especially not in utterly substanceless ICO tokens, with no basis in anything whatsoever, being traded like hotcakes because they're the exciting new item and for no other reason. At least tulips are pretty.

Bitcoin itself, as an ideology fundamentally at odds with reality based on a technology that reached its limits in 2015, will keep lurching from crisis to crisis. Internecine conflicts will remain the order of the day, with partisans wielding DDOS attacks, death threats and the deployment of Craig Wright as some sort of expert. The price will rise and fall dizzyingly, though realising it as actual money will still be strangely problematic; exchanges will continue to be hacked on a monthly basis. People will continue to lament "if only I'd bought in 2011, I'd be rich!" – though if they *had* bought in 2011, they'd have lost it in Mt. Gox. Cooler heads will wonder just how much longer this can be kept going.

The one constant is: new ideas in finance bring new starry-eyed naïfs, and new predators. New technologies will keep being used as an excuse to put an extra layer of flim-flam over old scams, in an ongoing historical reenactment of the reasons for each and every financial regulation.

There will be more promises of free riches in the future, and more asset bubbles. All of this will happen again. The hook may be different, but wishful thinking and scammers to prey on it are eternal.

Everything to do with cryptocurrencies and blockchains is the domain of fast-talking conmen. If anyone tries to sell you on either, kick them in the nuts and run.

# Further reading

*Memoirs of Extraordinary Popular Delusions and the Madness of Crowds* by Charles Mackay was first published in 1841 and remains the best book available on economic bubble thinking.

Nathaniel Popper's book *Digital Gold: Bitcoin and the Inside Story of the Misfits and Millionaires Trying to Reinvent Money* (Harper, ISBN 0062362496) is an excellent history of Bitcoin and the players to 2014.

David Golumbia's *The Politics of Bitcoin: Software as Right-Wing Extremism* (University of Minnesota Press, ISBN 978-1-4529-5381-6) is a short but very useful academic survey that traces just where the Bitcoin cluster of crank political and economic ideas sprang from.

Izabella Kaminska regularly discusses Bitcoin and blockchains (and "Blockchain") in the *Financial Times*, both in the main paper and her blog at *FT Alphaville*. I've found her work a powerful and effective antidote to business bafflegab Blockchain hype in real-world usage. Matt Levine does similarly good work at *Bloomberg*.

The RationalWiki.org article on Bitcoin has come along nicely since 2011. Unlike Wikipedia, we're not constrained from calling a spade a bloody shovel. In the US, we're tax deductible as a 501(c)3 educational charity! Though not accepting Bitcoin at this time.

# Acknowledgements

Elizabeth Sandifer suggested in October 2016 that I write a book about "Why Bitcoin Is Stupid or something," thus lodging a sort of parasitical book-writing worm in my brain. (This was *supposed* to be a quick 15,000-word rant before lunch.) Always ready with a motivational quip, like "if you're expecting a sense of accomplishment when you finish, you'll want to stop that."

Arkady Rose put up with me talking nothing but cryptos for months and beta-read the early drafts. I knew I was onto something when I watched Arkady laugh out loud all through the second half of The DAO section. Intermittently cursing Elizabeth for causing them to be subjected to this.

My beta readers, fact-checkers and nit-pickers, particularly on Facebook, for essential ideas, research leads critiques and saving my backside repeatedly, including (amongst many others): Fiona Apps, Julian Ardente, Matthew Ardill, Lee Baldwin, Sean Barrett, Asaf Bartov, Jacinta Blackbourne, Karen Boyd, Abigail Brady, Ricky Buchanan, Roger Burton-West, Vitalik Buterin, David Cake, Katie Chan, Alex Clarke, Doug Clow, D Coetzee, Peter H. Coffin, Lindsay Duff, Stephen Early, Daniel Ericsson, "DOS," "Facehammer," Caroline Ford, Jeff Franzmann, Sabitha Furiosa, Andrew Garrett, David Goh, Steve Gustafson, John Hawkes-Reed, Nigel Heffernan, Deana Holmes, Lizzy Jeffcoat, Axel Johnston, Sam Kelly, Andrew Ketrow, Alli Kirkham, Jola Kupferer, Lev Lafayette, Stuart Lamble, Charles Lieberman, Joe Lynn, Pauline Martindale, Chris McKenna, Brian McNeil, MegaZone, Tristan Miller, Edward Morbius, Tom Morris, Wayne Nix, Corwyn O'Domhnaill, Caoimhín Ó Gormáin, Hartley Patterson, Phy Phor, Larry Pieniazek, Drew Robertson, Madjai Sabine, Gunther Schmidl, Stefanie Schulte, C. J. Scott, Rebecca Scott, Dan Sheppard, James Skinner, Helen Smith, Humberto Solis, Andrew Stallings, Tim Starling, Jorge Stolfi, Joe Thompson, Sarah Thompson, Hester Tidcombe, Nicholas Turnbull, Django Upton, Alison Wheeler and the acerbic cryptocurrency skeptics of Reddit /r/buttcoin and Something Awful YOSPOS.

Alli Kirkham for her applied excellence not only in art (I *love* Scared Business Guy) but graphic design. Go commission her.

All my friends who fervently encouraged me through my progress reports.

Thank you, I couldn't have done it without all of you. It's amazing how much work even a short book is.

# About the author

David Gerard is a Unix system administrator by day. His job includes keeping track of exciting new technologies and advising against the bad ones. He was previously an award-winning music journalist, and has blogged about music at Rocknerd.co.uk since 2001. He is a volunteer spokesman for Wikipedia, and is on the board of the RationalMedia Foundation, host of skeptical wiki RationalWiki. His website is davidgerard.co.uk. He lives in east London with his spouse Arkady and their daughter. Until he reinstalled the laptop they were on, he was the proud owner of six Dogecoins.

# Glossary

**Address:** a long number which you can send Bitcoins to and from. Can only have coins sent from it using the matching *key*. Together they make a key pair in *public key cryptography*.

**Anarcho-capitalism:** the ideology that a complete absence of government is essential, and property rights, which are paramount, will still function without it. Bitcoin ideology shares a lot of its ideas and jargon.

**ASIC:** Application-Specific Integrated Circuit – a silicon chip to do a single specific job. In *mining*, the only power-efficient way to mine bitcoins.

**Bitcoin:** The greatest invention in the history of humanity.

**Blockchain:** The other greatest invention in the history of humanity.

**BTC:** the usual abbreviation for Bitcoin as a currency unit. Less common abbreviation: *XBT*.

**Bubble:** in economics, when an asset is hugely popular for no discernible reason. The key factor is investors buying in the hope of selling to later investors. Bubbles always pop. Bitcoin has had two major bubbles, in 2013 and 2017.

**Cold wallet:** Bitcoin private keys kept offline. Could be *wallet* software on a computer that's not online, could be keys on a USB stick, could be printed out on paper.

**Consensus model:** How you choose who gets to write the next block. Bitcoin uses *Proof of Work*, which is hugely wasteful.

**Craig Wright:** Not *Satoshi Nakamoto*.

**Crypto:** in this context, an abbreviation for *cryptocurrency* or *crypto asset*. In non-cryptocurrency use, the term is short for "cryptography."

**Crypto asset:** the general class of cryptographic things that aren't necessarily *cryptocurrency*, but can be traded like it, *e.g.* tokens in a smart contract running on Ethereum.

**Cryptocurrency:** Bitcoin and its various copies.

**Cypherpunks:** a mailing list for cryptography enthusiasts against the forces of oppression, *i.e.* any government anywhere. Heavy on the *anarcho-capitalism*. Most of the ideas that became Bitcoin started here.

**DAO:** see *The DAO*.

**Dapp:** a "distributed application," a fancy name for a *smart contract* in Ethereum.

**Darknet:** sites only available via *Tor*, where you can buy illegal goods and services using a *cryptocurrency*.

**Distributed ledger technology:** a euphemism for *blockchain*.

**DRM:** Digital Rights Management, an entertainment industry term for "that song I just bought and downloaded won't play." Music industry blockchain applications frequently involve a version of it, whether by name or not.

**Ethereum:** a cryptocurrency whose value proposition is *smart contracts*. Arguably the first popular smart contract platform.

**Exchange:** A site to buy or sell cryptos for actual money. Many offer fancy ~~gambling~~ trading facilities. May not get hacked this month.

**Fiat:** Actual proper money that normal people buy things with. Only Bitcoiners ever use this term when talking about actual money in casual conversation.

**FPGA:** Field-Programmable Gate Array – a silicon chip you can program to perform your function. In *mining*, the step between graphics cards and *ASICs*.

**Front-running:** in stock markets, for a broker or *exchange* to act on insider information. The crypto version is to take a particularly good trade and execute it yourself, before executing the customer's order. This is illegal on conventional regulated security exchanges.

**Gold standard:** an economy with a known and limited money supply. Bitcoin aims to implement this digitally and hark back to the days countries backed their currency with actual piles of gold.

**GPU:** Graphics Processing Unit, the bit of a computer graphics card that computes video game pixels very fast and can also compute *hashes* very fast. Used to be the favoured *mining* method for Bitcoin before being superseded by *FPGAs* and *ASICs;* remains the favoured mining method for *Ethereum*.

**Hal Finney:** *Cypherpunks* mailing list participant and Bitcoin's first beta tester. Died 2014. Some people think he was *Satoshi Nakamoto*.

**Hash:** a quickly-computed check value on a chunk of data. If two chunks of data have the same hash, it's usual to assume they are identical. A hash is strong if it's all but impossible to guess the data from its hash, or to construct a chunk of data that has the same hash as another chunk of data. Bitcoin *mining* relies on this.

**Hashpower:** How much computing power you can apply to *mining* to guess a *hash* that gets you the bitcoin reward for adding a block to the *blockchain*.

**Hot wallet:** software that keeps copies of the private keys for your bitcoins, and sends transactions to and receives them from the Bitcoin network (and eventually, when they go into a block, the blockchain).

**ICO:** Stands for "Initial Coin Offering" or "Initial Crowdfunding Offering", but in practice means a token that is speculated upon just because speculators can. Hugely popular in the second bubble.

**Immutable:** something that cannot be changed. The *blockchain* is considered immutable, as any change would change the hashes and be immediately evident.

**Key:** a number which works like the PIN of a Bitcoin *address*. This is the one secret thing you must control if you "have" a bitcoin.

**KYC/AML:** Know Your Customer/Anti-Money Laundering rules, which any crypto *exchange* wanting to deal in hard currencies, particularly US dollars, needs to follow.

**Margin call:** when you need to pay back your *margin trading* loan.

**Margin trading:** taking a loan from your brokerage to buy a security; lets you buy more than the value of the assets you have to hand. Could be hoping for the security to go up or down. Can pay off hugely, but is risky (especially with cryptos). *Short selling* is a form of margin trading.

**Mark Karpelès:** Owner of *Mt. Gox* when it collapsed. Did nothing wrong.

**Mempool:** the "memory pool," in the memory of a computer running a Bitcoin node, where unconfirmed transactions pile up.

**Merchant:** actual shopkeeper selling legal goods or services, who probably doesn't accept Bitcoin.

**Merkle tree:** an ordered collection of transactions, each hashed against the *hash* of previous transactions; this makes it very quick to verify the tree of transactions is the one you think it is. Bitcoin and blockchains rely on a Merkle tree to verify everything is in order and hasn't been tampered with. Invented by Ralph Merkle in 1979.

**Mining:** literally wasting electricity as a competitive sport to make new bitcoins.

**Mixer:** somewhere to send your bitcoins in order to obscure their history.

**Mt. Gox:** The largest bitcoin *exchange* in the run-up to the 2013 *bubble;* collapsed soon after, sending $400 million in bitcoins up in smoke.

**Nick Szabo:** Cypherpunks list participant. Came up with the idea of *smart contracts.* Proposed Bitgold, one of the precursor ideas to Bitcoin.

**Oracle problem:** how to tell a smart contract when a real-world event it depends on has happened, without requiring human judgement.

**Painting the tape:** where traders collude to make it look like there's activity in a security, or to push the price up. The Willy and Markus bots, running on *Mt. Gox* in the days before the 2013 crash, were a notorious Bitcoin example.

**Permissioned blockchain:** a private blockchain allowing only known participants. Allows the use of a simpler *consensus model.*

**PGP:** "Pretty Good Privacy," a program to sign or encrypt messages using *public key cryptography.*

**PHP:** A programming language for websites. Very easy to make a site in, and very easy to make an insecure site in if you don't know what you're doing. Quite a lot of Bitcoin *exchanges* started with someone thinking "I know PHP, how hard could running a Bitcoin exchange be?"

**Ponzi:** an "investment programme" in which earlier investors are paid with the contributions of later investors. Named after Charles Ponzi, who was famous for such schemes in the 1920s. A more general category of fraud than "pyramid scheme."

**Private blockchain:** another term for *permissioned blockchain.*

**Proof of Stake:** A *consensus model* that is far less wasteful than *Proof of Work,* by just declaring that thems what has, gets.

**Proof of Work:** A *consensus model* in which you compete to write the next block in the *blockchain* by just wasting more electricity than everyone else. This is as terrible as it sounds.

**Public key cryptography:** a way to sign or encrypt messages using two keys, one to encode and one to decode. Either can decode messages encoded with the other. Bitcoin uses this to authenticate transactions as having been sent by you: you sign them with the address's private key, and this is verified with the address (which is the public key).

**Ransomware:** Computer malware that locks up your Windows PC and demands bitcoins to unlock it.

**Roger Ver:** early Bitcoin advocate and *anarcho-capitalist.*

**Satoshi Nakamoto:** the pseudonym used by the creator of Bitcoin. Disappeared in 2011; nobody knows who he was.

**SEC:** The U.S. Securities and Exchange Commission, the government agency that enforces securities law and regulates the industry. Its mission statement is: "protect investors; maintain fair, orderly, and efficient markets; facilitate capital formation."

**Short selling, shorting:** selling a security you don't own in the hope it will go down and you can buy to cover what you sold. A form of *margin trading.*

**Smart contract:** a contract implemented as a computer program that triggers given particular conditions.

**The DAO:** a *smart contract* for a Distributed Autonomous Organization, intended to operate as an automated venture capital firm. The most famous smart contract ever, as the world's largest crowdfunding at the time, gathering $150 million. Hacked shortly after launch, losing $50 million and splitting *Ethereum* into two currencies.

**Tor:** The Onion Router, a method to browse the web anonymously. Development is substantially sponsored by the US government, both for their own use and to help dissidents in oppressive countries. (Even as the NSA doesn't like it at all.) Also favoured by Internet trolls and *darknet* users.

**Tulip:** a pretty flower, and the subject of the 1637 *bubble* known as "tulip mania," one of the first well-documented bubbles.

**Turing complete:** when a computer or computer language is sophisticated enough that it can theoretically solve any problem that any other computer can … given enough memory and time. You often don't want this, because it makes it harder to prove mathematical correctness when you really need to be certain, *e.g.* in a *smart contract.*

**Wallet:** anywhere you keep the private keys to your bitcoins. Can be a *hot wallet* or *cold wallet.*

**XBT:** An abbreviation for Bitcoin as a currency unit. More proper (currency units that aren't for a specific country are supposed to start with X) but less common than *BTC.*

# Index

158

# Notes

1   Satoshi Nakamoto. "Bitcoin: A Peer-to-Peer Electronic Cash System".
    Bitcoin.org, 31 October 2008.

2   For all the technical detail, see: "Developer Guide". Bitcoin.org.

3   Bitcoin power consumption was estimated at between 0.1 and 10 GW average
    by June 2014; Ireland consumed around 3 GW by this time. O'Dwyer and
    Malone. "Bitcoin Mining and its Energy Footprint". Presented at ISSC 2014 /
    CIICT 2014, Limerick, June 26–27 2014. The most detailed estimate I've seen
    for 2017 puts it at about half a 2017 Ireland: "Bitcoin Energy Consumption
    Index". *Digiconomist* (blog).

4   Alan Feuer. "The Bitcoin Ideology". *New York Times*, 14 December 2013.

5   Eric M. Jackson. *The PayPal Wars: Battles With eBay, the Media, the Mafia, and the
    Rest of Planet Earth*. World Ahead Publishing, 2004. Chapter 1.

6   Charlie McCombie. "Bitcoin Predecessor – Liberty Reserve Founder Receives
    20-Year Prison Sentence". *CoinTelegraph*, 10 May 2016.

7   David Chaum. "Blind signatures for untraceable payments". *Advances in
    Cryptology: Proceedings of Crypto*. **82** (3) *1982, pp. 199–203*.

8   David Chaum. "Security without Identification: Transaction Systems to Make
    Big Brother Obsolete". *Communications of the ACM*, **28** *(10)* 1985, pp. 1030–1044.

9   Tim May. "The Crypto Anarchist Manifesto". Written 1988, posted 22
    November 1992.

10  Satoshi Nakamoto. Comment on "Transactions and Scripts: DUP HASH160 …
    EQUALVERIFY CHECKSIG". Bitcointalk.org Bitcoin Forum > Bitcoin >
    Development & Technical Discussion, 18 June 2010.

11  Satoshi Nakamoto. Comment on "They want to delete the Wikipedia article".
    Bitcointalk.org Bitcoin Forum > Bitcoin > Bitcoin Discussion, 20 July 2010.

12  Gwern Branwen. "Dai/Nakamoto emails". Gwern.net. Version of 8 March
    2017.

13  The conspiracy theory is most famously set out in Robert Welch. "The Truth In
    Time". *American Opinion*, November 1966.

14  David Ferguson. "Ron Paul slams stability of U.S. dollar and Bitcoin in pro-gold
    rant". *Raw Story*, 23 April 2013.

15  Satoshi Nakamoto. "Bitcoin open source implementation of P2P currency".
    P2P Foundation forums, 11 February 2009.

16  Jonathan Thornburg. "Bitcoin v0.1 released". *Cryptography and Cryptography Policy*
    mailing list, 17 January 2009.

17  Ludwig von Mises. *Human Action*. Part One: Human Action. Chapter II. The
    Epistemological Problems of the Sciences of Human Action. 1. Praxeology and
    History, p32.

18  Elizabeth Sandifer. *Neoreaction a Basilisk*. Eruditorum Press, 2017.

19  Ben Best. "Bitcoin and Austrian Economics". *Bitcoin Magazine*, 27 August 2014.

20  "Myths". Bitcoin Wiki. Accessed 20 September 2016.

21  "The Story Of When Buttcoin.org Sold Out And How Butterfly Labs Turned It (And Other Sites) Into A Product Marketing Machine". Buttcoin Foundation, 14 November 2014.

22  Peter Yeh. "FTC Shuts Down Bogus Bitcoin Op Butterfly Labs, Says 'Buttcoin'". *Animal*, 25 September 2014.

23  "Securing your wallet". Bitcoin Wiki.

24  "About PayPal", version of 26 December 2014. "almost 10 million payments for our customers per day."

25  "Visa Inc. at a Glance". Visa, June 2015.

26  Western Union. "Notice of 2014 Annual Meeting of Stockholders, Proxy Statement and 2013 Annual Report." p2.

27  Christopher Malmo. "A Single Bitcoin Transaction Takes Thousands of Times More Energy Than a Credit Card Swipe". *Motherboard*, 7 March 2017.

28  Godfreee. "If I was looking to sell big (or relatively big) amounts of BTC on the OTC market, what would be my best option?". Reddit /r/bitcoinmarkets, 15 February 2015.

29  Zhoutong. "Bitcoin Wealth Distribution (Bitcoinica data)". Bitcointalk.org Bitcoin Forum > Bitcoin > Bitcoin Discussion, 6 November 2011.

30  Steven Englander, Citigroup, quoted in Joe Wiesenthal. "How Bitcoin Is Like North Korea". *Business Insider*, 12 January 2014.

31  Dorit Ron, Adi Shamir. "Quantitative Analysis of the Full Bitcoin Transaction Graph". Cryptology ePrint Archive, Report 2012/584, 25 October 2012.

32  Hal Finney. "Bitcoin 0.1 released". *Cryptography and Cryptography Policy* mailing list, 10 January 2009.

33  Jim Epstein. "The Secret, Dangerous World of Venezuelan Bitcoin Mining: How cryptocurrency is turning socialism against itself". *Reason*, January 2017.

34  Kamilia Lahrichi. "Growing number of Venezuelans trade bolivars for bitcoins to buy necessities". *The Guardian*, 16 December 2016.

35  Kamilia Lahrichi. "Argentina's Bitcoin Scene Booms". *International Finance Magazine*, July-September 2015.

36  Mariana Zuñiga. "Bitcoin 'mining' is big business in Venezuela, but the government wants to shut it down". *Washington Post*, March 10 2017.

37  Nathaniel Popper. "S.E.C. Rejects Winklevoss Brothers' Bid to Create Bitcoin E.T.F." *New York Times*, 10 March 2017.

38  Leisha Chi. "Bitcoin digital currency hits three-year high of $1,000". BBC News, 3 January 2017.

39  "LocalBitcoins Volume (Venezuela)". Coin Dance.

40  Nick Szabo. "The Greek financial mess; and some ways Bitcoin might help". *Unenumerated* (blog), 3 July 2015.

41  ZhouTonged. "Cyprus Anthem (Swedish House Mafia – Don't You Worry Child)". YouTube, 5 May 2013.

42  Charles Mackay, *Memoirs of Extraordinary Popular Delusions and the Madness of Crowds*. Full text is available in various formats on Project Gutenberg.

43  Martti Malmi. Twitter, 15 January 2014.

44   Laszlo. "Pizza for bitcoins?" Bitcointalk.org Bitcoin Forum > Economy > Marketplace, 18 May 2010.

45   historyofbitcoin.org

46   Jean-Paul Rodrigue. "Stages in a Bubble". *The Geography of Transport Systems*, 2008.

47   "A Bit expensive: Bitcoin's record price looks like a bubble". *Daily Chart, The Economist*, 19 March 2013.

48   Peter Ford. "Why the Chinese can't get enough of Bitcoin – despite bank ban". *Christian Science Monitor*, 6 December 2013.

49   Rick Falkvinge. "The Target Value For Bitcoin Is Not Some $50 Or $100. It Is $100,000 To $1,000,000". *Falkvinge on Liberty* (blog), 6 March 2013.

50   A good short overview: Marie Vasek, Tyler Moore. "There's No Free Lunch, Even Using Bitcoin: Tracking the Popularity and Profits of Virtual Currency Scams". *International Conference on Financial Cryptography and Data Security*. Springer Berlin Heidelberg, 2015.

51   Gwern Branwen. "Bitcoin is Worse is Better: Irreversible transactions: meta-scams".

52   "Scams: Doubling money". RuneScape Wikia.

53   "Operators of Bitcoin Mining Operation Butterfly Labs Agree to Settle FTC Charges They Deceived Consumers". Federal Trade Commission (press release), 18 February 2016.

54   Cyrus Farivar. "Digging for answers: The 'strong smell' of fraud from one Bitcoin miner maker". *Ars Technica*, 22 April 2014.

55   A good, though technical, explanation: Jon Matonis. "BitZino And The Dawn Of 'Provably Fair' Casino Gaming". *Forbes* (contributor blog), 31 August 2012.

56   keepinquiet. "How 999dice.com is stealing your coins, and exactly why you won't believe me". Bitcointalk.org Bitcoin Forum > Economy > Trading Discussion > Scam Accusations, 7 February 2015.

57   Jeffrey Tucker. "A Theory of the Scam". *Beautiful Anarchy* (blog), 2 January 2015.

58   Unclescrooge. "[shame thread]The sorry and thank you Pirateat40 thread". Bitcointalk.org Bitcoin Forum > Economy > Marketplace > Lending > Long-term offers, 17 August 2012.

59   Mageant. "Bitcoin Killer App: High Yield Investments". Bitcointalk.org Bitcoin Forum > Bitcoin > Bitcoin Discussion, 22 July 2012.

60   Vitalik Buterin. "Ponzi schemes: The Danger of High Interest Savings Funds". *Bitcoin Magazine*, 31 May 2012.

61   Adrianne Jeffries. "Suspected multi-million dollar Bitcoin pyramid scheme shuts down, investors revolt". *The Verge*, 27 August 2012.

62   yochdog. "The pirate speaks". Bitcointalk.org Bitcoin Forum > Economy > Marketplace > Lending, 17 September 2012.

63   Killhamster. "pirateat40: It became Bill Cosby coins". Buttcoin Foundation, 5 March 2014.

64   Jason Siebert. "SEC v. SHAVERS". 21 July 2014.

65  *Securities and Exchange Commission v. Shavers et al*, U.S. District Court, Eastern District of Texas, No. 13-00416.

66  Jonathan Stempel. "Judge Awards $40.7 Million in SEC Case Over Bitcoin Ponzi Scheme". *Recode*, 19 September 2014.

67  "Manhattan U.S. Attorney And FBI Assistant Director Announce Securities And Wire Fraud Charges Against Texas Man For Running Bitcoin Ponzi Scheme". Department of Justice, U.S. Attorney's Office, Southern District of New York (press release), 6 November 2014.

68  Nate Raymond. "Texan gets one-and-a-half years in prison for running bitcoin Ponzi scheme". *Reuters*, 21 July 2016.

69  Justin O'Connell. "Lawyer Reveals Details About the Man Behind Bitcoin's $4.5 Million Ponzi Scheme". *Motherboard*, 18 December 2015.

70  "Risk of Bitcoin Hacks and Losses Is Very Real". *Reuters*, 29 August 2016.

71  Kyt Dotson. "Third Largest Bitcoin Exchange Bitomat Lost Their Wallet, Over 17,000 Bitcoins Missing". *SiliconAngle*, 1 August 2011.

72  Coinabul. "10 Questions with Zhou Tong". *Bitcoin Magazine*, 30 May 2012.

73  Vitalik Buterin. "Bitcoinica Stolen From … Again". *Bitcoin Magazine*, 17 July 2012.

74  Stan Higgins. "BitPay Sues Insurer After Losing $1.8 Million in Phishing Attack". *CoinDesk*, 17 September 2015.

75  P. H. Madore. "AllCrypt Bitcoin Exchange Clears the Air". *CryptoCoinsNews*, 26 March 2015.

76  Duncan Riley. "Bitcoin stolen from lending startup Loanbase in alleged hack". *SiliconAngle*, 9 February 2016.

77  Stan Higgins. "Cryptsy CEO Stole Millions From Exchange, Court Receiver Alleges". *CoinDesk*, 11 August 2016.

78  Kraken Exchange. "No compromise. CloudFlare issue. Some users may need to update their browsers to support SNI. IE/XP users may need to enable TLS 1.1/1.2". Twitter, 26 January 2016.

79  Matthew Prince. "@krakenfx let's get the facts straight. Credit card provided for payment expired. After 3 warnings you were downgraded to a free account". Twitter, 27 January 2016.

80  Roger Ver. "Roger Ver on MTGOX Bitcoin exchange". YouTube, 17 July 2013.

81  Roger Ver. Comment on "[VIDEO] Roger Ver says he is sorry about MTGOX". Bitcointalk.org Bitcoin Forum > Economy > Marketplace > Service Discussion, 26 February 2014.

82  Kdawson. "Bitcoin Releases Version 0.3". *Slashdot*, 11 July 2010.

83  Martti Malmi. "I'm Martti Malmi, early bitcoin developer and the original founder of the Bitcointalk.org forums, AMA!" Bitcoin.com forums, 18 November 2015.

84  Cyrus Farivar. "Why the head of Mt. Gox Bitcoin exchange should be in jail". *Ars Technica*, 1 August 2014.

85  Jake Adelstein, Nathalie-Kyoko Stucky. "Behind the Biggest Bitcoin Heist in History: Inside the Implosion of Mt. Gox". *Daily Beast*, 19 May 2016.

86   Ryan Selkis. "Leaked Mt. Gox Document Linked to Consulting Firm Mandalah". *CoinDesk*, 27 February 2014.

87   A good technical explanation: Ed Felten. "Understanding Bitcoin's transaction malleability problem". *Freedom to Tinker* (blog), 12 February 2014.

88   Nermin Hajdarbegovic. "Price Drops as Mt. Gox Blames Bitcoin Flaw for Withdrawal Delays". *CoinDesk*, 10 February 2014.

89   Christian Decker, Roger Wattenhofer. "Bitcoin Transaction Malleability and MtGox". arXiv:1403.6676v1 [cs.CR], 26 March 2014.

90   Ken Shirriff. "The programming error that cost Mt Gox 2609 bitcoins". March 2014.

91   Kim Nilsson. "The missing MtGox bitcoins". WizSec, 19 April 2015.

92   Comma in original. Roger Ver. "Both Anne Frank, and Ross Ulbricht created dark markets to help people hide from violent oppressors who were trying to hurt peaceful people." Twitter, 16 July 2016.

93   Mike Power. "Online highs are old as the net: the first e-commerce was a drugs deal". *The Guardian*, 19 April 2013.

94   Satoshi Nakamoto. Comment on "Re: Porn". Bitcointalk.org Bitcoin Forum > Economy > Economics > adf, 23 September 2010.

95   "Join the Tor Challenge". Electronic Frontier Foundation.

96   Yasha Levine. "Almost Everyone Involved in Developing Tor was (or is) Funded by the US Government". *Pando*, 16 July 2014.

97   Even Facebook has one, for users in heavily-filtered countries. Alec Muffett. "1 Million People use Facebook over Tor". *Facebook over Tor* (official page), Facebook, 22 April 2016.

98   Gwern Branwen. "Silk Road: Theory & Practice". 11 July 2011, updated 8 March 2016.

99   Adrian Chen. "The Underground Website Where You Can Buy Any Drug Imaginable". *Gawker*, 1 June 2011.

100  Andy Greenberg. "Prosecutors Trace $13.4M in Bitcoins From the Silk Road to Ulbricht's Laptop". *Wired*, 29 January 2015.

101  This phrase was popularised by the *New York Times* in January 2014 (David Segal. "Eagle Scout. Idealist. Drug Trafficker?" *New York Times*, 18 January 2014), but the earliest usage I've found is a comment from Yves Smith, founder of the blog *Naked Capitalism*, on his reposting of Yanis Varoufakis. "Bitcoin and the Dangerous Fantasy of 'Apolitical' Money". 23 April 2013.

102  *United States v. Ross William Ulbricht*, S1 14 Cr. 68 (KBF), Opinion & Order, Document 173, 1 February 2015.

103  Joseph Cox. "How Did the FBI Find the Silk Road Servers, Anyway?" *Motherboard*, 3 October 2014.

104  Joe Mullin. "Judge in Silk Road case gets threatened on Darknet". *Ars Technica*, 22 October 2014.

105  Machkovech, Sam. "Notorious 8chan 'subboard' has history wiped after federal judge's doxing". *Ars Technica*, 12 February 2015.

106  Poly Paradyme. "Interview with Lyn Ulbricht About Upcoming Silk Road Appeal". *Coinivore*, 25 November 2015.

107 Andy Greenberg. "In Silk Road Appeal, Ross Ulbricht's Defense Focuses on Corrupt Feds". *Wired*, 12 January 2016.

108 *United States of America v. Ulbricht*, 15-1815-cr, Document 177, page 122, 31 May 2017.

109 Eileen Yu. "Anonymous website disappears with $100M in Bitcoin". *ZDNet*, 5 December 2013.

110 Andy Greenberg. "Feds Seize Silk Road 2 in Major Dark Web Drug Bust". *Wired*, 6 November 2014.

111 Satoshi Nakamoto. Comment on "A few suggestions". Bitcointalk.org Bitcoin Forum > Bitcoin > Development & Technical Discussion, 12 December 2009.

112 For a collection of firetrap home mining rigs: Killhamster. "Mining Rig Megapost". Buttcoin Foundation, 13 February 2015.

113 "Miner Who Reported Brain Damage Tells All". *Bitcoin Mining Accidents* (blog), 11 June 2011.

114 *e.g.*, Yusho Cho. "Bitcoin trade volume hits record in November". *Nikkei Asian Review*, 18 December 2016.

115 Gautham. "Bitmain Responds to Controversy Surrounding its Upcoming 140,000 kW Mining Center". *NewsBTC*, 4 November 2016.

116 "Google Data Center FAQ, Part 2". *Data Center Knowledge*.

117 "Bitcoin Mining Pools". BitcoinChain.com, 16 March 2017.

118 Yuji Nakamura, Lulu Yilun Chen. "Bitcoin Miners Signal Revolt Amid Sluggish Blockchain". *Bloomberg*, 13 March 2017.

119 Ittay Eyal, Emin Gün Sirer. "How A Mining Monopoly Can Attack Bitcoin". *Hacking Distributed* (blog), 16 June 2014.

120 Cyrus Farivar. "Bitcoin pool GHash.io commits to 40% hashrate limit after its 51% breach". *Ars Technica*, 16 July 2014.

121 Kenny Spotz. "An Interview With Jeffrey Smith, CIO of GHash.io". *Bitcoin Magazine*, 23 June 2014.

122 Thomas Fox-Brewster. "Craig Wright Claims He's Bitcoin Creator Satoshi – Experts Fear An Epic Scam". *Forbes* (staff blog), 2 May 2016.

123 Gwern Branwen. "Happy birthday, Satoshi Nakamoto". Reddit /r/bitcoin, 5 April 2014.

124 *e.g.*, Dominic Frisby. "The Search for Satoshi". *CoinDesk*, 8 November 2014.

125 Gwern Branwen. "Blackmail fail".

126 Leah McGrath Goodman. "The face behind Bitcoin". *Newsweek*, 6 March 2014.

127 Ryan Nakashima. "Man said to create bitcoin denies it". AP *The Big Story*, 7 March 2014.

128 Satoshi Nakamoto. Comment on "Bitcoin open source implementation of P2P currency". P2P Foundation forums, 7 March 2014.

129 Matt Clinch. "'Real' bitcoin creator: 'I am not Dorian Nakamoto'". CNBC, 7 March 2014.

130 Leslie Kaufman, Noam Cohen. "Newsweek Returns to Print and Sets Off a Bitcoin Storm". *New York Times*, 7 March 2014, pB3.

131 "Newsweek's Statement on the Bitcoin Story". *Newsweek*, 7 March 2014.

132 "Craig Steven Wright claims to be Satoshi Nakamoto. Is he?" *The Economist*, 2 May 2016.

133 Craig S. Wright. "The quantification of information systems risk: A look at quantitative responses to information security issues" (doctoral thesis). Charles Sturt University, February 2017.

134 "craig-wright-cpunks-1996.txt". Cryptome.

135 Craig Wright. "Looking for people interested in starting a new revolution in payments". *Cracked, inSecure and Generally Broken* (blog), 4 February 2011.

136 Craig S. Wright. "LulzSec, Anonymous … freedom fighters or the new face of evil?" *The Conversation*, 9 August 2011.

137 apoefjmqdsfls. "According to the Mtgox leaks from early 2014, our brand new 'Satoshi' Craig Wright bought 17.24 bitcoins at a rate of $1198 each". Reddit /r/bitcoin, 4 May 2016.

138 Ian Grigg. "Triple Entry Accounting". 25 December 2005.

139 Sarah Jeong. "Satoshi's PGP Keys Are Probably Backdated and Point to a Hoax". *Motherboard*, 9 December 2015.

140 "Hotwire Preemptive Intelligence Pty Limited (Administrators Appointed) ACN 164 068 348 ('the Company'): Circular to Creditors". McGrathNicol, 26 May 2014.

141 "The DeMorgan Ltd Group of Companies to receive up to $54 million from AusIndustry R&D tax rebate scheme: Australia's fastest Top500 HPC is dedicated to Cryptocurrency and smart contract research". DeMorgan Ltd (press release), 11 May 2015.

142 Andrew O'Hagan. "The Satoshi Affair". *London Review of Books*, **38** *(13)* pp7-28, 30 June 2016. Reprinted in O'Hagan's 2017 book The Secret Life: Three True Stories (Faber, ISBN 0571335845).

143 Andy Greenberg, Gwern Branwen. "Bitcoin's Creator Satoshi Nakamoto Is Probably This Unknown Australian Genius". *Wired*, 8 December 2015.

144 Sam Biddle and Andy Cush. "This Australian Says He and His Dead Friend Invented Bitcoin". *Gizmodo*, 8 December 2015, updated 2 May 2016.

145 Leah McGrath Goodman. "@kashhill We all got it. It was being shopped around fairly aggressively this autumn. @nathanielpopper @a_greenberg". Twitter, 10 December 2015.

146 "Tulip-Trust-Redacted". *Gizmodo*.

147 Purported redacted transcript of interviews with Australian Tax Office auditor.

148 Transcript: Richy_T. Comment on "WikiLeaks: SGI super-computer 'letter' removed from Craig Wright's company 'cloudsoft'". Reddit /r/bitcoin, 10 December 2015.

149 Kashmir Hill. "Who is the hacker that outed Craig Wright as the creator of Bitcoin? Maybe Craig Wright himself". *Fusion*, 9 December 2015.

150 Aimee Chanthadavong. "SGI denies links with alleged bitcoin founder Craig Wright". *ZDNet*, 11 December 2015.

151 "TOP500 List November 2015". *Top500*, November 2015.

152 Elle Hunt and Paul Farrell. "Reported bitcoin 'founder' Craig Wright's home raided by Australian police". *The Guardian*, 9 December 2015.

153 Leo Shanahan. "ATO's fraud squad probes Bitcoin 'creator' Craig Wright". *The Australian*, 21 January 2016.

154 Gavin Andresen. "Satoshi". 2 May 2016.

155 Jon Matonis. "How I Met Satoshi". 2 May 2016.

156 Gavin Andresen. Comment on "Gavin, can you please detail all parts of the signature verification you mention in your blog". Reddit /r/btc, 2 May 2016.

157 Dan Kaminsky. "Validating Satoshi (Or Not)". 2 May 2016.

158 Byron Kaye, Jeremy Wagstaff. "Australian 'bitcoin founder' quietly bidding for patent empire". *Reuters*, 20 June 2016.

159 Byron Kaye, Jeremy Wagstaff. "Bitcoin's 'creator' races to patent technology with gambling tycoon". *Reuters*, 2 March 2017.

160 Jeremy Wagstaff, Byron Kaye. "Exclusive: Company behind bitcoin 'creator' sold to private investors". *Bloomberg*, 24 April 2017.

161 "NCHAIN LIMITED Company number 09823112". Companies House, 2 May 2017.

162 "Jon Matonis Joins Blockchain Pioneer nChain as Vice President of Corporate Strategy". nChain (press release), 2 May 2017.

163 Peter Todd (@petertoddbtc). "If that scammer tries to sue me I'm going to lol so hard…" Twitter, 30 June 2017.

164 Kristy Kruithof, Judith Aldridge, David Décary Hétu, Megan Sim, Elma Dujso, Stijn Hoorens. "Internet-facilitated drugs trade: An analysis of the size, scope and the role of the Netherlands". Rand Corporation, 2016.

165 Herb Weisbaum. "Ransomware: Now a Billion Dollar a Year Crime and Growing". NBC News, 9 January 2017.

166 "Frequently Asked Questions: Find answers to recurring questions and myths about Bitcoin". bitcoin.org.

167 Giuseppe Pappalardo, T. Di Matteo, Guido Caldarelli, Tomaso Aste. "Blockchain Inefficiency in the Bitcoin Peers Network". arXiv:1704.01414, 5 April 2017.

168 45sbvad. "Stress Test Recap". Reddit /r/bitcoin, 30 May 2015.

169 "Bitcoin Network Capacity Analysis – Part 5: Stress Test Analysis". TradeBlock, 16 June 2015.

170 Jacob Donnelly. "Updated: Bitcoin Network Still Backlogged With Tens of Thousands of Unconfirmed Transactions, Causing Delays". *Bitcoin Magazine*, 7 July 2015.

171 Grace Caffyn. "Bitcoin Node Numbers Fall After Spam Transaction 'Attack'". *CoinDesk*, 15 October 2015.

172 Jordan Pearson. "Is Bitcoin Under Attack?" *Motherboard*, 1 March 2016.

173 Izabella Kaminska. "The currency of the future has a settlement problem". *FT Alphaville* (blog), *Financial Times*, 17 May 2017.

174 Nathaniel Popper. "A Bitcoin Believer's Crisis of Faith". *New York Times*, 14 January 2016.

175 Kyle Soska, Nicolas Christin. "Measuring the Longitudinal Evolution of the Online Anonymous Marketplace Ecosystem". *Proceedings of the 24th USENIX Security Symposium*, 12-14 August 2015.

176 Gwern Branwen. "Dark Net Market archives, 2011-2015". Internet Archive, 12 July 2015.

177 Gwern Branwen. "Black-Market Archives". 1 December 2013, updated 3 November 2016.

178 Andy Greenberg. "The Silk Road's Dark-Web Dream is Dead". *Wired*, 14 January 2016.

179 AlphaBay_mod. "AlphaBay will add Ethereum to its payment options". Reddit /r/alphabaymarket, 18 March 2017.

180 "Extortion virus code gets cracked". BBC News, 1 June 2006.

181 "Why the police virus was so effective". *PC Advisor*, 26 February 2013.

182 "New Ransomware Study Explores 'Customer Journey' of Getting Your Files Back". F-Secure, 18 July 2016.

183 "Ransomware risk could cripple British businesses with many not ready, while others stockpiling bitcoins to pay up". Citrix (press release), June 2016.

184 Chris Mayers. "Ransomware in the UK: One year on". Citrix blog, 6 June 2017. Citrix give the questions and sample selection criteria in the comments.

185 "Incidents of Ransomware on the Rise: Protect Yourself and Your Organization". FBI, 29 April 2016.

186 "Telstra Cyber Security Report 2017". Telstra, 30 March 2017.

187 According to an NHS IT worker I know, who spent his Saturday reimaging PCs.

188 Jemima Kelly."Bitcoin's murkier rivals line up to displace it as cybercriminals' favourite". *Reuters*, 18 May 2017.

189 Fahmida Y. Rashid. "How to tell if you've been hit by fake ransomware". *InfoWorld*, 29 April 2016.

190 "Manhattan U.S. Attorney Announces Charges Against Two Florida Men for Operating an Underground Bitcoin Exchange". FBI (press release), 21 July 2015.

191 *Digital Gold* by Nathaniel Popper, chapter 31, notes leading lights of Bitcoin expressing this precise worry at the Bitcoin Pacifica conference in 2014: "For the sake of Bitcoin as a whole, there were many who worried that the consumers who were buying things online through Bitpay were pushing the price of Bitcoin down; generally when online retailers accepted Bitcoins they immediately sold them off for dollars, creating a downward pressure on the overall price."

192 The_Mastor. "I tried to order a deck of Cards Against Humanity using Bitcoins but was surprised by this negative response. What do you guys think?" Reddit /r/bitcoin, 30 July 2013.

193 Max Temkin. "'They just prefer the imaginary debt-based money their slavemasters issue via the central banks.' Yes I use it to buy groceries." Twitter, 30 July 2013.

194 "Hi Max! In what way do you believe Bitcoin to be an 'imaginary currency'". *Maxistentialism* (blog), 30 July 2013.

195 Henry Belot. "How many people actually use bitcoin in Canberra?" *Canberra Times*, 3 September 2014.

196 Grace Caffyn. "WordPress: WeH aven't Given Up on Bitcoin". *CoinDesk*, 25 February 2015.

197 Andrea Wood. "Bitcoin Donations to Mozilla: 17 Days In". Mozilla: View Source Fundraising (blog), 8 December 2014.

198 Nuno Menezes. "Mozilla Study Shows Bitcoin has Negative Impact on Donations". *Bitcoinist*, 20 August 2015.

199 David Gerard. "Wikimedia did rather better with bitcoin than Mozilla: ~$140k in the first week, ~$80k since for a total of ~$220k so far in the year we've accepted it". Reddit /r/buttcoin, 7 August 2015. (I asked the Wikimedia fundraising department and posted the answer to Reddit.)

200 mwalker. "Re: [Wikimedia-l] Let's accept Bitcoin as a donation method". wikimedia-l mailing list, 8 January 2014.

201 Shawn Knight. "Overstock does nearly $1 million in Bitcoin sales in first month". *TechSpot*, 21 February 2014.

202 Hal M. Bundrick. "Overstock: Bitcoin Sales 'Disappointing' but 'Nobody's Complaining'". *Inside Bitcoins*, 16 December 2014.

203 Pete Rizzo. "Overstock Reports Over $100k in Crypto Losses for Q1 2015". *CoinDesk*, 24 June 2015.

204 Whollyhemp. Comment on "I work for a large sports nutrition company, I'm trying to help them implement a bitcoin pay option. Do you think it'll show short term usage?" Reddit /r/bitcoin, 9 April 2015.

205 Whollyhemp. Comment on "Payment processors need to offer consumer friendly exchange rates if they want people to buy things with bitcoin". Reddit /r/bitcoin, 5 April 2015.

206 Whollyhemp. "This is why you don't anger Bitcoiners". Reddit /r/buttcoin, 1 May 2015.

207 Whollyhemp. Comment on "/u/jstolfi goes the way of whollyhemp after death threats from scientologists". Reddit /r/buttcoin, 20 September 2015.

208 Pete Rizzo. "Bitcoin Continues March to Mainstream at St Petersburg Bowl Game". *CoinDesk*, 27 December 2014.

209 Kevin Collier. "The real high-stakes game waged at the Bitcoin Bowl". *The Kernel*, 11 January 2015.

210 Pete Rizzo. "Bitcoin Bowl Merchants See Tech's Big Picture, But Few Sales". *CoinDesk*, 2 January 2015.

211 Kevin Collier. "The great Bitcoin experiment that failed". *Daily Dot*, 2 January 2016.

212 *Linux User & Developer*, a 2007 issue I've yet to track down (and Steve doesn't have).

213 sde1000. btcmerch. github.io.

214 Garrick Hileman. "State of Bitcoin and Blockchain 2016: Blockchain Hits Critical Mass". *CoinDesk*, 28 January 2016. "Chinese yuan denominated trading represented 95% of total exchange volume."

215 "How do I verify a US bank account?" Coinbase Support.

216 Lauren Razavi. "The Struggle Between Bitcoin Traders and British Banks". *Motherboard*, 13 January 2015.

217 Paul Smith. "ACCC investigating banks' closure of bitcoin companies' accounts". *Australian Financial Review*, 19 October 2015.

218 Charles Bovaird. "On High Seas of Bitcoin Trading, Whales Still Make Waves". *CoinDesk*, 14 September 2016.

219 J. P. Buntinx. "GDAX Bitcoin Price Briefly Crashes to US$0.06 after System Maintenance". *NewsBTC*, 16 April 2017.

220 "Bitcoin bots bought millions in the last days of Mt Gox". *The Guardian*, 29 May 2014.

221 Bobby Lee. "Reminder: Chinese bitcoin spot exchanges OKCoin and Huobi are faking a majority of their trading volume". *Bitcoin Futures Guide* (blog), 28 March 2016.

222 Justina Lee and Emma Dai. "Bitcoin Extends Loss After China's Central Bank Warns Investors". *Bloomberg*, 9 January 2017.

223 Jorge Stolfi. "Trading volume at the main Chinese exchanges steadily dropping for the last 10 days. Should be zero tomorrow". Reddit /r/buttcoin, 17 January 2017.

224 "China Bitcoin Exchanges Halt Withdrawals After PBOC Talks". *Bloomberg*, 10 February 2017.

225 "Nigerians, Everything you need to know about the MMM Bitcoin scam". *Nigeria Today*, 19 October 2016.

226 *e.g.*, *CoinDesk*'s Bitcoin Price Index.

227 Cryptowatch. https://cryptowat.ch/

228 David Shares. "New details emerge about Bitfinex's history amid hacking probe". *Bitcoin.com*, August 3, 2016.

229 elux. Comment on "[Daily Discussion] Sunday, October 04, 2015". Reddit /r/bitcoinmarkets, 4 October 2015.

230 "Bitfinex Completes AlphaPoint Integration". AlphaPoint (press release), 28 April 2015.

231 elux. Comment on "[Daily Discussion] Sunday, October 04, 2015". Reddit /r/bitcoinmarkets, 4 October 2015.

232 Using Pay-to-Script Hash, which is part of Bitcoin. How it works at BitGo: Mike Belshe. "P2SH Safe Address". BitGo.

233 Lulu Yilun Chen, Yuji Nakamura. "Hacked Bitcoin Exchange Says Users May Share $68 Million Loss". *Bloomberg*, 5 August 2016.

234 "Bitfinex Interim Update". Bitfinex blog, 6 August 2016.

235 Edmundedgar. Comment on "Bitfinex and Wells Fargo: what did Bitfinex know and when did they know it?" Reddit /r/buttcoin, 15 May 2017.

236 "BFX Token Terms". Bitfinex, August 2016.

237 "BFX Margin Trading Is Live". Bitfinex blog, 31 August 2016.

238 "BFX token to iFinex equity conversion update". Bitfinex blog, 24 September 2016.

239 "Bitfinex Recovery Right Tokens". Bitfinex blog, 11 October 2016.

240 "RRT Exchange Trading Enabled". Bitfinex blog, 11 October 2016.

241 Zane Tackett. "Bitfinex: Update Regarding Security Audit, Financial Audit, And More". Reddit /r/bitcoinmarkets, 17 August 2016.

242 "Interim update". Bitfinex blog, 17 August 2016, as updated 4 May 2017.

243 Giancarlo Devasini. "Message to the individual responsible for the Bitfinex security incident of August 2, 2016". Bitfinex blog, 21 October 2016.

244 Andrew Quentson. "Bitfinex's Hacked Bitcoins Are on the Move; 5% Recovery Bounty Offered". *CryptoCoinsNews*, 27 January 2017.

245 "100% Redemption of Outstanding BFX Tokens". Bitfinex Announcements, 3 April 2017.

246 Yuji Nakamura. "Inside Bitfinex's Comeback From a $69 Million Bitcoin Heist". *Bloomberg*, 17 May 2017.

247 "USD Withdrawals Update". Bitfinex Announcements, 12 May 2017.

248 "Phil Potter 'Solved' Banking Problems in the past by 'Shifting' Corporate entities w/ new accounts." YouTube.

249 *iFinex Inc., BFXNA Inc., BFXWW Inc., and Tether Limited vs. Wells Fargo and Company, Wells Fargo Bank, N.A.* U.S. District Court, Northern District of California, No. 17 Civ. 1882.

250 Stan Higgins. "Bitfinex Withdraws Lawsuit Against Wells Fargo". *CoinDesk*, 12 April 2017.

251 Mark Karpelès. Comment on "Mark Karpelès offers counsel and consolation to his spiritual brethren at Bitfinex". Reddit /r/buttcoin, 9 April 2017.

252 "Pausing Wire Deposits to Bitfinex". Bitfinex Announcements, 17 April 2017.

253 "Outflows to Customers". Bitfinex Announcements, 20 April 2017.

254 CoinDesk price.

255 Voogru. Comment on "[Daily Discussion] Tuesday, May 23, 2017". Reddit /r/bitcoinmarkets, 23 May 2017.

256 Joseph Young. "South Korean Bitcoin Exchange Suffers $5 Million Hack, Issues Bitfinex-Like Tokens". *CryptoCoinsNews*, 28 April 2017.

257 Unclescrooge. "[shame thread]The sorry and thank you Pirateat40 thread". Bitcointalk.org Bitcoin Forum > Economy > Marketplace > Lending > Long-term offers, 17 August 2012.

258 Unclescrooge. "Unclescrooge 1-week deposit program at 2%/week". Bitcointalk.org Bitcoin Forum > Economy > Marketplace > Lending > Long-term offers, 13 September 2012.

259 Andrew Quentson. "Bitfinex's Founder Seemingly Tried to Start a Ponzi Scheme". *Cryptocoins News*, 8 June 2016.

260 "DafuqCoin, the first malware coin." *Cryptocurrency Times* (blog), 4 May 2014.

261 The code that injects the rootkit is jawdroppingly blatant and worth reading. Richiela. "READ ME NOW! – dafuqcoin is a trojan – pool operators/exchanges beware". Bitcointalk.org Bitcoin Forum > Alternate cryptocurrencies > Altcoin Discussion, 22 April 2014.

262 Clay Michael Gillespie. "Dogecoin Leaders Present Evidence that CEO of Troubled Bitcoin Exchange Moolah Is Long-Time Scammer". *CryptoCoinsNews*,

16 October 2014.

263 Duncan Riley. "Mintpal scammer Ryan Kennedy arrested in U.K. over theft of 3,700 Bitcoins". *SiliconAngle*, 23 February 2015.

264 "Ryan Kennedy convicted of three counts of rape against three women". Crown Prosecution Service (press release), 26 May 2016.

265 "Man charged with fraud and money-laundering". Avon and Somerset Constabulary (press release), 29 June 2017.

266 Joseph Frusetta (sporadicallyjoe). "DogecoinOnTheMoon: We're going to reach the lunar surface next year!" Reddit /r/dogecoin, 3 August 2016.

267 Mohland. "[Important] I'm taking dogetipbot to a server farm upstate". Reddit /r/dogecoin, 8 May 2017.

268 Vitalik Buterin. "Dagger-Hashimoto".

269 "Ethash Design Rationale". Ethereum Wiki, 21 March 2015.

270 e.g., Oimie. "Bought too many Gpus – Delimma". Reddit r/ethermining, 24 June 2017.

271 "Ethereum Average BlockSize Chart". Etherscan.io.

272 "Ethereum Uncle Count And Rewards Chart". Etherscan.io.

273 "Ethereum Transaction Chart". Etherscan.io.

274 Joseph Young. "Ethereum Launches; But Leaked Chat Says Project Needs 'Years More'". *CoinTelegraph*, 1 August 2015.

275 *e.g.*, Vlad Zamfir. "About my tweet from yesterday …" 5 March 2017.

276 "Vitalik's Quantum Quest". *Bitcoin Error Log* (blog), 16 August 2016.

277 Jordan Ash. "Why Turing Machines are Quantum." *Noospheer* (blog), 4 September 2013. "If successful, it will have applications ranging from cryptography to finance, energy, medical care and beyond."

278 Vitalik Buterin. Comment on "Why does Greg Maxwell and many others from Bitcoin Core not respect Vitalik?" Reddit /r/btc, 16 August 2016.

279 Amy Castor. "Ethereum 'Tokens' Are All the Rage. But What Are They Anyway?" *CoinDesk*, 17 June 2017.

280 DigixDAO.

281 "Crowdfunding Whitepaper". The Golem Project, November 2016.

282 Alyssa Hertig. "ICO Insanity? $300 Million Gnosis Valuation Sparks Market Reaction". *CoinDesk*, 25 April 2017.

283 A survey of the top 8 ICOs at the time: Lyle Cantor. "A Tour of the Ethereum Token Bubble". 18 June 2017.

284 *e.g.*, Emin Gün Sirer, Phil Daian. "Bancor Is Flawed". *Hacking, Distributed* (blog), 19 June 2017.

285 "SNT Creation and Status Project Creation Conditions: Explanatory Note & Governance Terms". status.im.

286 Edan Yago. "Ads on Taxis – Is EOS.io the PETS.com of ICO?" Twitter, 11 July 2017.

287 "EOS.IO Technical White Paper". EOS.IO.

288 Red Li. "EOS Triples in 2 Days, Making Yunbi Top Tier Exchange With Over 230k BTC Volume". 8BTC, 3 July 2017.

289 "Frequently Asked Questions". EOS.IO.

290 "EOS Token Purchase Agreement". EOS.IO.

291 CoinHoarder. "EOS – Asynchronous Smart Contract Platform - (Dan Larimer of Bitshares/Steem)". Bitcointalk.org Bitcoin Forum > Alternate cryptocurrencies > Altcoin Discussion, 6 May 2017.

292 "Decentralized content publishing". press.one.

293 Red Li. "Exchanges Alerts ICO Scams and Illegal Fundraising in China Punishable by Death". *8BTC*, 26 June 2017.

294 Cindy23. "ICO Investors Lose All Their Money When Reads a Whitepaper Encoded with Viruses". *8BTC*, 30 June 2017.

295 Stan Higgins. "ICO Blues: Status Raises $64 Million (So Far) But Leaves Buyers Waiting". *CoinDesk*, 20 June 2017.

296 Charles Mackay, *Memoirs of Extraordinary Popular Delusions and the Madness of Crowds*, chapter 2. "The South-Sea Bubble".

297 https://ponzico.win/

298 Josh Cincinnati. "PonzICO: Let's Just Cut To The Chase". 12 May 2017.

299 "Ethereum Account 0x1ce7986760ade2bf0f322f5ef39ce0de3bd0c82b Info". Etherscan.io.

300 Nick Szabo. "Smart Contracts". 1994.

301 Nick Szabo. "Towards a digital and private common law". *Unenumerated* (blog), 13 May 2007.

302 *e.g.*, Samar Warsi. "This Company Wants to Give You a Divorce on the Blockchain". *Motherboard*, 30 May 2017.

303 An extreme example: Akin Fernandez. "Are you a Bitcoin denialist?" *The Finanser* (blog), 18 September 2016.

304 *e.g.*, Stephen Tual, later of The DAO. Gian Volpicelli. "Smart Contracts Sound Boring, But They're More Disruptive Than Bitcoin". *Motherboard*, 16 February 2015.

305 Vitalik Buterin. "Thinking About Smart Contract Security". *Ethereum Blog*, 19 June 2016.

306 Matt Levine. "Crossing the Rubicon and Gagging Shkreli". *Bloomberg*, 5 July 2017.

307 Maxim Lott. "New tech promises government-proof prediction markets". Fox News Tech, 20 August 2015.

308 Szabo used this example in his original Smart Contracts paper, and reiterated it in "Formalizing and Securing Relationships on Public Networks". *First Monday* **2** (9), 1 September 1997. ISSN 13960466.

309 Nick Szabo. "The dawn of trustworthy computing". *Unenumerated* (blog), 11 December 2014.

310 Christian Reitwiessner. "Security Alert – Solidity – Variables can be overwritten in storage". *Ethereum Blog*, 1 November 2016.

311 King of the Ether: "An Ethereum contract, living on the blockchain, that will make you a King or Queen, might grant you riches, and will immortalize your name."

312 Nick Szabo. "A Formal Language for Analyzing Contracts". 2002.

313 Nicola Atzei, Massimo Bartoletti, Tiziana Cimoli. "A survey of attacks on Ethereum smart contracts". 6th International Conference on Principles of Security and Trust (POST), European Joint Conferences on Theory and Practice of Software, April 2017.

314 Muneeb Ali. "Solarstorm: A security exploit with Ethereum's Solidity language, not just the DAO". Blockstack Blog, 21 June 2016.

315 Zikai Alex Wen and Andrew Miller. "Scanning Live Ethereum Contracts for the 'Unchecked-Send' Bug". *Hacking Distributed* (blog), 16 June 2016. "Upon inspection, not one of the Solidity programs that passed our heuristic check actually applied the recommended best-practice of testing the callstack directly."

316 Peter Vessenes. "Ethereum Contracts Are Going To Be Candy For Hackers". *Blockchain, Bitcoin and Business* (blog), 18 May 2016.

317 Martin Holst Swende. "Ethereum contract security: An Ethereum Roulette". 14 August 2015.

318 Ethererik. "GovernMental's 1100 ETH jackpot payout is stuck because it uses too much gas". Reddit /r/ethereum, 26 April 2016.

319 "Post-Mortem Investigation (Feb 2016)". *King of the Ether.*

320 "Hi! My name is Rubixi. I'm a new Ethereum Doubler. Now my new home – Rubixi.tk". Bitcointalk.org Bitcoin Forum > Alternate cryptocurrencies > Marketplace (Altcoins) > Service Announcements (Altcoins), 11 April 2016.

321 Vitalik Buterin. "Live example of 'underhanded solidity' coding on mainnet". Reddit /r/ethereum, 10 April 2016.

322 brockchainbrockshize. Comment on "Attacker has withdrawn all ETC from DarkDAO on the unforked chain". Reddit /r/ethereum, 25 July 2016.

323 The DAO front page 22 June 2016. Yes, that's *after* the hack.

324 Dino Mark, Vlad Zamfir, Emin Gün Sirer. "A Call for a Temporary Moratorium on The DAO". *Hacking, Distributed* (blog), 27 May 2016.

325 Peter Vessenes. "More Ethereum Attacks: Race-To-Empty is the Real Deal". *Blockchain, Bitcoin and Business* (blog), 9 June 2016.

326 Stephen Tual. "No DAO funds at risk following the Ethereum smart contract 'recursive call' bug discovery". blog.slock.it, 12 June 2016.

327 Stephen Tual. "Why the DAO robber could very well return the ETH on July 14th". *Ursium* (blog), 9 July 2016.

328 Tjaden Hess, River Keefer, Emin Gün Sirer. "Ethereum's DAO Wars Soft Fork is a Potential DoS Vector". *Hacking, Distributed* (blog), 28 June 2016.

329 Stephen Tual. "Vitalik Buterin, Gavin Wood, Alex van De Sande, Vlad Zamfir announced amongst exceptional DAO Curators". blog.slock.it, 25 April 2016.

330 Tracy Alloway. "An experiment". 19 January 2017.

331 Richard Waters. "Bitcoin 2.0 gives the dreamers focus — but only without the hype". *Financial Times*, 4 December 2014.

332 Earliest sighting I've found: JP Koning. "Why the Fed is more likely to adopt bitcoin technology than kill it off". 14 April 2013.

333 Jeremy Cuomo. "Making Blockchain Ready for Business: Increase trust, accountability, and transparency across your business networks". IBM, 2016. The author link in the text is to a deleted Wikipedia article.

334 Rodger Oates, Raghavasuresh Samudrala. "Industrialisation of Distributed Ledger Technology in Banking and Financial Services". TechUK, 20 June 2016.

335 A good survey of the blockchain in relation to this: Jim Greco. "Wall Street Loves the Blockchain". *Tabb Forum*, 2 June 2017.

336 Oliver Ralph. "Reinsurers turn to blockchain technology". *Financial Times*, 16 May 2016.

337 *e.g.*, "How to find out who owns a property or a piece of land". *Land and property blog*, HM Land Registry, 10 October 2013.

338 Izabella Kaminska. "Tuna blockchains and Chilean Seabass". *FT Alphaville* (blog), *Financial Times*, 6 September 2016.

339 "From shore to plate: Tracking tuna on the blockchain". Provenance, 15 July 2016.

340 Matt Levine. "Executive Pay and Blood Trouble". *Bloomberg View*, 11 July 2016.

341 The *only* useful past work on this I've found: "Distributed Ledger Technology & Cybersecurity: Improving information security in the financial sector". European Union Agency for Network and Information Security, 18 January 2017. My only qualms are that it uses as references *Zero Hedge* and *Breitbart News*.

342 Vitalik Buterin. "On Public and Private Blockchains". *Ethereum Blog*, 7 August 2015.

343 Izabella Kaminska. "Exposing the 'If we call it a blockchain, perhaps it won't be deemed a cartel?' tactic". *FT Alphaville* (blog), *Financial Times*, 11 May 2015.

344 Izabella Kaminska. "Introducing the 'mutualised database'". *FT Alphaville* (blog), *Financial Times*, 6 October 2016.

345 Izabella Kaminska. "Blockchains? Where we're going, we don't need blockchains". *FT Alphaville* (blog), *Financial Times*, 26 August 2016.

346 "Bitcoin Venture Capital". *CoinDesk*, 9 February 2017.

347 *e.g.*, David Kaaret. "Is Your Firm Ready for Blockchain-Based Trade Processing?". MarkLogic blog, 5 December 2016.

348 James Eyers. "ASX builds blockchain for Australian equities". *Sydney Morning Herald*, 22 January 2016.

349 Jackie Range. "New Australian Securities Exchange chief defends blockchain plans". *Financial Times*, 5 September 2016.

350 Chanticleer. "Blockchain option for ASX clearing in limbo". *Australian Financial Review*, 12 January 2017.

351 Clive Boulton. "Banks find blockchain hard to put into practice [also supply chain]". *Hyperledger-Requirements-WG* (mailing list), 12 September 2016.

352 Viraj Kamat. "Questions on the Next Consensus Architecture". *Hyperledger technical-discuss* (mailing list), 1 September 2016.

353 Kadhim Shubber. "Banks find blockchain hard to put into practice". *Financial Times*, 12 September 2016.

354 Richard Lumb, Accenture. "Downside of Bitcoin: A Ledger That Can't Be Corrected". *Dealbook* (blog), *New York Times*, 9 September 2016.

355 Morgan Grey. "Azure Blockchain as a Service Update #5". Microsoft Azure blog, 29 February 2016.

356 Pete Rizzo. "Linux, IBM Share Bold Vision for Hyperledger Project, a Blockchain Fabric for Business". *CoinDesk*, 11 February 2016.

357 "Projects". Hyperledger.org.

358 Digital Asset. "Moving Hyperledger to the Linux Foundation". 2016.

359 Intel Corporation. "Sawtooth Lake: Docs: Introduction". 2016.

360 Chain Core Docs. "Operating a blockchain".

361 Visa Inc. "Visa B2B Connect: New kid on the blockchain: Visa and Chain to bring improved international B2B payments to market". October 2016.

362 Richard Gendal Brown. "Introducing R3 Corda™: A Distributed Ledger Designed for Financial Services". *R3 Blog*, 5 April 2016. "Notice some of the key things: firstly, we are not building a blockchain."

363 "Distributed ledger technology: Blackett review". Government Office for Science, 19 January 2016.

364 GO-Science. "Block chain technology". YouTube, 19 January 2016.

365 Mike Masnick. "How ASCAP Takes Money From Successful Indie Artists And Gives It To Giant Rock Stars". *TechDirt*, 26 March 2012.

366 Olivia Brown. "ASCAP's Live Performance Royalties No Longer Reserved For Top Touring Acts". Future of Music Coalition, 9 October 2012.

367 Ben Sisario. "Going to the Ends of the Earth to Get the Most Out of Music". *New York Times*, 8 June 2015.

368 *See* Wikipedia: Sony BMG copy protection rootkit scandal.

369 "Fair Music: Transparency and Payment Flows in the Music Industry". Rethink Music, Berklee Institute for Creative Entrepreneurship, July 2015.

370 Chris Cooke. "PRS confirms Global Repertoire Database 'cannot' move forward, pledges to find 'alternative ways'". *Complete Music Update*, 10 July 2014.

371 *e.g.,* Andy Edwards. "The UK music industry tried to agree a 'transparency code' for streaming royalties. It collapsed – here's why". *Music Business Worldwide*, 26 February 2017

372 George Howard. "Imogen Heap's Mycelia: An Artists' Approach for a Fair Trade Music Business, Inspired by Blockchain". *Forbes* (contributor blog), 17 July 2015.

373 *e.g.,* Hatching Amazing. "Part 1: How we tried to buy Imogen Heap's song on Ethereum". 24 January 2016.

374 Everett Rosenfield. "Company leaves New York, protesting 'BitLicense'". CNBC, 11 June 2015.

375 andrewkeys. "Purchase Imogen Heap's 'Tiny Human' with Ether on ConsenSys project, Ujo, the decentralized peer-to-peer music platform!" Reddit /r/ethereum, 3 October 2015.

376 "Emerging from the Silence". Ujo Music blog, 29 August 2016.

377 Ben Ratliff. "Is Bandcamp the Holy Grail of Online Record Stores?" *New York Times*, 19 August 2016.

378 Horace Dedlu. "iTunes users spending at the rate of $40/yr". Asymco, 12 May 2013.

379 Stuart Dredge. "Spotify now processes 'nearly 1bn streams every day'". *Music Ally*, 22 July 2015.

380 "Music on the Blockchain". Blockchain for Creative Industries Research Cluster, Middlesex University, July 2016.

381 Petter Ericson, Peter Harris, Elizabeth Larcombe, Turo Pekari, Kelly Snook, Andrew Dubber. "#MTFLabs: Blockchain". 23 August 2016.

382 Jeremy Silver. "Blockchain or the Chaingang?" *CREATe Working Paper Series*, May 2016. DOI: 10.5281/zenodo.51326.

383 "The Blockchain: Change everything forever". Furtherfield, October 2016. Transcript, video. Another that would greatly benefit from being narrated by Philomena Cunk.

384 John Lahr. "Berklee's Open Music Initiative". *Music Business Journal*, Berklee College of Music, September 2016.

385 Gideon Gottfried. "How 'the Blockchain' Could Actually Change the Music Industry". *Billboard*, 5 August 2015.

386 Kevin Cruz. "PeerTracks: Paradigm Shift In Music World". *Bitcoin Magazine*, 22 October 2014.

387 Benji Rogers. "How Blockchain Can Change the Music Industry (Part 2)". Rethink Music, Berklee Institute for Creative Enterprise, 24 February 2016.

388 Rhian Jones. "Revelator gets $2.5m funding led by Exigent Capital". *Music Business Worldwide*, 30 August 2016.

389 "TAO Network Partners With Boogie Shack Music Group to Offer Blockchain Solution". TAO Network (press release), 22 August 2016.

390 Zach LeBeau. "Anatomy of SingularDTV's CODE (Centrally Organized Distributed Entity)". 9 August 2016.

391 "SNGLS Creation and S-DTV CODE Smart Project Creation Conditions: Explanatory Note & Governance Terms". SingularDTV, September 2016.

392 "The SingularDTV (S-DTV) CODE Summary Overview: For a Blockchain Film & Television Entertainment Studio & Distribution Portal, with a Smart Contract Rights Management Platform". SingularDTV, 22 July 2016.

393 Zach LeBeau. "An Ethereum Journey to Decentralize All Things: From the DAO to the CODE (Centrally Organized Distributed Entity)". 11 July 2016.

394 Tim Ingham. "Spotify revenues topped $3bn in 2016, with losses above $330m – report". *Music Business Worldwide*, 18 May 2017.